WHAT'S COOKING
wok & stir-fry

Siân Davies

DP
DEMPSEY
PARR

First published in Great Britain in 1998 by
Dempsey Parr
13 Whiteladies Road
Clifton
Bristol
BS8 1PB

ISBN: 1-84084-179-6 (hdbk)
ISBN: 1-84084-220-2 (ppbk)

Printed in Italy

Produced by Haldane Mason, London

Acknowledgements
Art Director: Ron Samuels
Editorial Director: Sydney Francis
Editorial Consultant: Christopher Fagg
Managing Editor: Jo-Anne Cox
Design: Digital Artworks Partnership Ltd
Photography: Iain Bagwell
Stylist: Rachel Jukes
Home Economists: Emma Patmore and Penny Stephens
Home Economists' Assistants: Nicky Deeley and Jane Stephens

Note
Cup measurements in this book are for American cups.
Tablespoons are assumed to be 15 ml. Unless otherwise stated,
milk is assumed to be full fat, eggs are medium
and pepper is freshly ground black pepper.

Contents

Introduction   4

Soups & Starters   6

Meat & Poultry   46

Fish & Seafood   124

Vegetarian Dishes   168

Rice & Noodles   214

Index   256

Introduction

Oriental cookery basically requires the use of a wok. If you have one then a whole array of wonderful dishes is open to you. It is worth buying a wok, rather than using a frying pan (skillet), for more satisfactory results when trying the delicious range of recipes which follow in this book.

Basically, a wok is a curved, shallow, bowl-like cooking implement which is made of metal and has either a single long, wooden handle or two looped handles at opposite sides of the pan. It comes in many sizes, but the most appropriate for a family is approximately 30-35 cm/12-14 inches in diameter. It may be made from stainless steel, cast iron or copper, the cast iron being the better choice as it retains heat more efficiently, especially when well-seasoned. There are numerous advantages to a wok over a frying pan (skillet). The convex shape means that food is easily moved around the wok and tossed (the basis of stir-frying) and cooks much more quickly. It can easily be tilted if required or rotated to reach ingredients easily.

Due to the curved sides of the wok, the heat rises and the whole wok becomes a hot cooking surface. It therefore conserves fuel and is perfect for quick cooking and stir-frying. Cleaning is no problem as there are no corners or edges in which food can become lodged.

USEFUL EQUIPMENT

There are several other pieces of equipment that will be useful with a wok. One of the most important in the Western kitchen is a **collar**. Basically this is a metal crown with angled sides and hollows which aids heat convection from our modern hobs and cooking rings. The wok sits in the collar and gives more even cooking than if the wok were simply placed on an electric ring. A **long-handled spatula** is useful for removing and cooking foods as the curved edge follows the curve of the wok. Be sure to buy one with a wooden handle to insulate your hands from the heat.

The wok is mainly used for stir-frying, but may also be used for deep-frying and steaming. A **frying strainer** or **shallow wire-meshed basket** is useful to remove foods from fat and a **steaming trivet** will convert your wok to a steamer.

Obviously a **lid** is essential for some wok cooking and should be domed and fitted snugly inside the wok to seal in the flavours during steaming. Many boxed wok sets contain all of these additional pieces of equipment as they are an essential part of wok cooking if it is to be used to its full potential.

USING YOUR WOK

Before using your wok it is essential to season it as with other pans. Wipe the wok inside and out with oiled kitchen paper and heat it to a high heat in the oven or on the hob. Remove the wok from the heat, allow it to cool and repeat this process several times to give a good coating – this will make it easier to clean and give it a non-stick coating. After the initial seasoning, the wok may be cleaned with soap and water, but it must be dried immediately if made of cast iron, to prevent it from rusting. Generally, the wok is simply wiped clean, and allowed to blacken with use. It is said that the blacker the wok, the better the cook, as it shows how frequently the wok is used.

STIR-FRYING

The wok is most widely used for stir-frying, a cooking method which originated in China, and remains the most recognised form of Chinese cooking. This method has spread throughout East Asia. In China it is called *Ch'au*, which primarily means one or a number of ingredients are sliced thinly and evenly and cooked in 1-2 tablespoons of fat. The food is stirred with long bamboo chopsticks or a spatula and seasonings and sauces are added.

Stir-frying is often done in stages. This allows foods which have longer cooking times to be stir-fried and removed and then returned to the wok at a later stage, and also for individual flavours to be kept distinct. The dish is always brought together at the end of cooking in the wok and served as a whole. Usually peanut or corn oil are used to fry the foods, but occasionally chicken fat and sometimes lard will be used for more delicate flavours.

There are different types of stir-frying which are described below:

Liu is wet frying with less vigorous stirring and more turning of the foods. A cornflour (cornstarch) and stock mixture is added with sugar, vinegar and soy sauce at the end of cooking for a delicious coating sauce.

Pao, or 'explosion', requires foods to be fried at the highest heat, and it is a very short, sharp method of cooking, usually lasting only 1 minute. Foods cooked in this way are generally marinated beforehand for flavour and tenderness.

WOK COOKING AROUND THE WORLD

Across the Far East woks are used in various guises for many dishes. In India, a large pan or *karahi* is used which sits over a hole in a brick or earth oven. This wok-like vessel is used for braising and frying, the infamous curry or *karahi* deriving its name from the pan. In Indonesia, a *wajan* or wok is used over wood or charcoal for curries, rice dishes and quick stir-fries – the same applies in Japan, Thailand, Singapore and Malaysia, all of which have been influenced by Chinese cooking. Even a Mongolian barbecue resembles a wok, being a convex iron griddle.

You will gather from the preceding information, that the wok and the stir-frying cooking method are both essential and unique to Asian and Far Eastern cooking, being swift, light, healthy and extremely versatile. The following recipes take you on a magical journey of the Far East, covering soups, starters, meat and poultry, fabulous fish dishes, vegetarian dishes and, of course, rice and noodles, the staples in these countries. So get out your wok and prepare yourself for the feast of flavours now open to you!

5

Soups & Starters

Soup is indispensable at Asian tables, especially in China, Japan, Korea and South East Asia. Chicken soup, for example, is sometimes served in China, Malaysia and Thailand for breakfast! However, it is generally eaten part way through a main meal to clear the palate for further dishes, but it is never served as a starter as in the Western world. There are many different types of delicious soups, both thick and thin and, of course, the clear soups which are often served with wontons or dumplings in them. In Japan, the clear soups are exquisite arrangements of fish, meat and vegetables in a clear broth.

Starters or snacks are drier foods in general, such as spring rolls, which come in many variations and shapes across the Far East. Satay is served in Indonesia, Malaysia and Thailand and other delights are wrapped in pastry, bread, rice paper or skewered for ease of eating. Again these are generally served as snacks in their native countries, but are frequent starters in Westernised restaurants.

The following chapter contains many delicious recipes for both soups and starters, all of which are the perfect way to begin a meal and whet the appetite for the delicious dishes that follow.

Spicy Chicken Noodle Soup

*This filling soup is filled with Thai flavours and colour
for a really attractive and hearty dish.*

Serves 4

INGREDIENTS

2 tbsp tamarind paste

4 red Thai chillies, finely chopped

2 cloves garlic, crushed

2.5 cm/1-inch piece Thai ginger,
   peeled and very finely chopped

4 tbsp fish sauce

2 tbsp palm sugar or caster
   (superfine) sugar

8 lime leaves, roughly torn

1.2 litres/2 pints/5 cups chicken stock

350 g/12 oz boneless chicken breast

100 g/3^{1}/$_{2}$ oz carrots, very thinly
   sliced

350 g/12 oz sweet potato, diced

100 g/3^{1}/$_{2}$ oz baby corn cobs, halved

3 tbsp fresh coriander (cilantro),
   roughly chopped

100 g/3^{1}/$_{2}$ oz cherry tomatoes, halved

150 g/5^{1}/$_{2}$ oz flat rice noodles

fresh coriander (cilantro), chopped,
   to garnish

1 Place the tamarind paste, Thai chillies, garlic, Thai ginger, fish sauce, sugar, lime leaves and chicken stock in a large preheated wok and bring to the boil, stirring constantly. Reduce the heat and cook for about 5 minutes.

2 Using a sharp knife, thinly slice the chicken. Add the chicken to the wok and cook for a further 5 minutes, stirring the mixture well.

3 Reduce the heat and add the carrots, sweet potato and baby corn cobs to the wok. Leave to simmer, uncovered, for 5 minutes, or until the vegetables are just tender and the chicken is completely cooked through.

4 Stir in the coriander (cilantro), cherry tomatoes and noodles. Leave the soup to simmer for about 5 minutes, or until the noodles are tender. Garnish and serve hot.

COOK'S TIP

Tamarind paste is produced from the seed pod of the tamarind tree. It adds both a brown colour and tang to soups and gravies. If unavailable, dilute molasses (dark muscovado) sugar or treacle with lime juice.

Crab & Sweetcorn Noodle Soup

Crab and sweetcorn are classic ingredients in Chinese cookery. Here egg noodles are added for a filling dish.

Serves 4

INGREDIENTS

1 tbsp sunflower oil
1 tsp Chinese five-spice powder
225 g/8 oz carrots, cut into sticks
150 g/5$^{1}/_{2}$ oz/$^{1}/_{2}$ cup canned or
   frozen sweetcorn
75 g/2$^{3}/_{4}$ oz/$^{1}/_{4}$ cup peas

6 spring onions (scallions), trimmed
   and sliced
1 red chilli, deseeded and very thinly
   sliced
2 x 200 g/7 oz can white crab meat
175 g/6 oz egg noodles

1.7 litres/3 pints/7$^{1}/_{2}$ cups fish stock
3 tbsp soy sauce

1 Heat the sunflower oil in a large preheated wok.

2 Add the Chinese five-spice powder, carrots, sweetcorn, peas, spring onions (scallions) and chilli to the wok and stir fry for about 5 minutes.

3 Add the crab meat to the wok and stir-fry the mixture for 1 minute.

4 Roughly break up the egg noodles and add to the wok.

5 Pour the stock and soy sauce into the mixture in the wok, bring to the boil, cover and leave to simmer for 5 minutes.

6 Transfer the soup to warm serving bowls and serve at once.

COOK'S TIP

Chinese five-spice powder is a mixture of star anise, fennel, cloves, cinnamon and Szechuan pepper.

COOK'S TIP

Use thin egg noodles for the best result in this recipe.

Spicy Thai Soup with Prawns (Shrimp)

*Lime is a classic flavouring in Thai cooking
which adds tartness to this soup.*

Serves 4

INGREDIENTS

2 tbsp tamarind paste
4 red Thai chilies, very finely chopped
2 cloves garlic, crushed
2.5 cm/1 inch piece Thai ginger,
    peeled and very finely chopped
4 tbsp fish sauce
2 tbsp palm sugar or caster
    (superfine) sugar

8 lime leaves, roughly torn
1.2 litres/2 pints/5 cups fish stock
100 g/3$^{1}/_{2}$ oz carrots, very thinly
    sliced
350 g/12 oz sweet potato, diced
100 g/3$^{1}/_{2}$ oz/1 cup baby corn cobs,
    halved

3 tbsp fresh coriander (cilantro),
    roughly chopped
100g/3$^{1}/_{2}$ oz cherry tomatoes, halved
225 g/8 oz fan-tail prawns (shrimp)

1 Place the tamarind paste,
chillies, garlic, ginger, fish
sauce, sugar, lime leaves and stock
in a large preheated wok. Bring to
the boil, stirring constantly.

2 Reduce the heat and add the
carrot, sweet potato and baby
corn to the mixture in the wok.

3 Leave the soup to simmer,
uncovered, for about
10 minutes, or until the vegetables
are just tender.

4 Stir the coriander, cherry
tomatoes and prawns
(shrimp) into the soup and heat
through for 5 minutes.

5 Transfer the soup to warm
serving bowls and serve hot.

COOK'S TIP

*Baby corn cobs have a sweet
fragrance and flavour. They are
available both fresh and canned.*

COOK'S TIP

*Thai ginger or galangal is a
member of the ginger family, but it
is yellow in colour with pink
sprouts. The flavour is aromatic
and less pungent than ginger.*

Coconut & Crab Soup

Thai red curry paste is quite fiery, but adds a superb flavour to this dish.
It is available in jars or packets from supermarkets.

Serves 4

INGREDIENTS

1 tbsp groundnut oil

2 tbsp Thai red curry paste

1 red (bell) pepper, deseeded and
   sliced

600 ml/1 pint/2^1/$_2$ cups coconut milk

600 ml/1 pint/2^1/$_2$ cups fish stock

2 tbsp fish sauce

225 g/8 oz canned or fresh white
   crab meat

225 g/8 oz fresh or frozen crab claws

2 tbsp chopped fresh coriander
   (cilantro)

3 spring onions (scallions), trimmed
   and sliced

1 Heat the oil in a large preheated wok.

2 Add the red curry paste and red (bell) pepper to the wok and stir-fry for 1 minute.

3 Add the coconut milk, fish stock and fish sauce to the wok and bring to the boil.

4 Add the crab meat, crab claws, coriander (cilantro) and spring onions (scallions) to the wok. Stir the mixture well and heat thoroughly for 2–3 minutes.

5 Transfer the soup to warm bowls and serve hot.

COOK'S TIP

Clean the wok after each use by washing it with water, using a mild detergent if necessary, and a soft cloth or brush. Do not scrub or use any abrasive cleaner as this will scratch the surface. Dry thoroughly with paper towels or over a low heat, then wipe the surface all over with a little oil. This forms a sealing layer to protect the surface of the wok from moisture and prevents it rusting.

COOK'S TIP

Coconut milk adds a sweet and creamy flavour to the dish. It is available in powdered form or in tins ready to use.

Chilli Fish Soup

Chinese mushrooms add an intense flavour to this soup which is unique.
Try to obtain them if you can, otherwise use opencap mushrooms, sliced.

Serves 4

INGREDIENTS

15 g/¹/₂ oz Chinese dried mushrooms
2 tbsp sunflower oil
1 onion, sliced
100 g/3¹/₂ oz/1¹/₂ cups mangetout
  (snow peas)

100 g/3¹/₂ oz/1¹/₂ cups bamboo
  shoots
3 tbsp sweet chilli sauce
1.2 litres/2 pints/5 cups fish or
  vegetable stock

3 tbsp light soy sauce
2 tbsp fresh coriander (cilantro)
450 g/1 lb cod fillet, skinned and
  cubed

1 Place the mushrooms in a large bowl. Pour over enough boiling water to cover and leave to stand for 5 minutes. Drain the mushrooms thoroughly. Using a sharp knife, roughly chop the mushrooms.

2 Heat the sunflower oil in a preheated wok. Add the onion to the wok and stir-fry for 5 minutes, or until softened.

3 Add the mangetout (snow peas), bamboo shoots, chilli sauce, stock and soy sauce to the wok and bring to the boil.

4 Add the coriander (cilantro) and cubed fish to the wok. Leave to simmer for 5 minutes or until the fish is cooked through.

5 Transfer the soup to warm bowls, garnish with extra coriander (cilantro) if wished and serve hot.

COOK'S TIP

There are many different varieties of dried mushrooms, but shiitake are best. They are not cheap, but a small amount will go a long way.

VARIATION

Cod is used in this recipe as it is a meaty white fish. For real luxury, use monkfish tail instead.

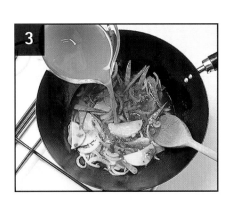

Hot & Sour Mushroom Soup

Hot and sour soups are found across South East Asia in different forms. Take care with the chillies and reduce the number added if you prefer a milder dish.

Serves 4

INGREDIENTS

2 tbsp tamarind paste

4 red Thai chilies, very finely chopped

2 cloves garlic, crushed

2.5 cm/1 inch piece of Thai ginger, peeled and very finely chopped

4 tbsp fish sauce

2 tbsp palm sugar or caster (superfine) sugar

8 lime leaves, roughly torn

1.2 litres/2 pints/5 cups vegetable stock

100 g/3½ oz carrots, very thinly sliced

225 g/8 oz button mushrooms, halved

350 g/12 oz shredded white cabbage

100 g/3½ oz fine green beans, halved

3 tbsp fresh coriander (cilantro), roughly chopped

100 g/3½ oz cherry tomatoes, halved

1 Place the tamarind paste, Thai chillies, garlic, Thai ginger, fish sauce, palm or caster (superfine) sugar, lime leaves and stock in a large preheated wok. Bring the mixture to the boil, stirring occasionally.

2 Reduce the heat and add the carrots, mushrooms, cabbage and green beans. Leave the soup to simmer, uncovered, for about 10 minutes, or until the vegetables are just tender.

3 Stir the coriander (cilantro) and cherry tomatoes into the mixture in the wok and heat through for 5 minutes.

4 Transfer the soup to warm bowls and serve hot.

COOK'S TIP

Tamarind is one of the ingredients that gives Thai cuisine its special sweet and sour flavour.

VARIATION

Instead of the white cabbage, try using Chinese leaves for a sweeter flavour. Add the Chinese leaves with the coriander (cilantro) and cherry tomatoes in step 3.

Thai-Style Spicy Sweetcorn Fritters

Cornmeal can be found in most supermarkets or health food shops.
Yellow in colour, it acts as a binding agent in this recipe.

Serves 4

INGREDIENTS

225 g/8 oz/³/4 cup canned or frozen sweetcorn
2 red Thai chillies, deseeded and very finely chopped

2 cloves garlic, crushed
10 lime leaves, very finely chopped
2 tbsp fresh coriander (cilantro), chopped

1 large egg
75 g/2³/4 oz/¹/2 cup cornmeal
100 g/3¹/2 oz fine green beans, very finely sliced
groundnut oil, for frying

1 Place the sweetcorn, chillies, garlic, lime leaves, coriander (cilantro), egg and cornmeal in a large mixing bowl, and stir to combine.

2 Add the green beans to the ingredients in the bowl and mix well, using a wooden spoon.

3 Divide the mixture into small balls. Flatten the balls of mixture between the palms of your hands to form rounds.

4 Heat a little groundnut oil in a preheated wok.

5 Cook the fritters, in batches, until brown and crispy on the outside, turning occasionally.

6 Transfer the fritters to warm serving plates and serve immediately.

COOK'S TIP

Kaffir lime leaves are dark green, glossy leaves that have a lemony-lime flavour. They can be bought from specialist Asian stores either fresh or dried. Fresh leaves impart the most delicious flavour.

COOK'S TIP

If using canned sweetcorn, drain thoroughly and then rinse and drain thoroughly again before use.

Vegetable Spring Rolls

There are many different versions of spring rolls throughout the Far East,
a vegetable filling being the classic.

Serves 4

INGREDIENTS

225 g/8 oz carrots
1 red (bell) pepper
1 tbsp sunflower oil, plus extra for
  frying
75 g/2³/₄ oz/³/₄ cup beansprouts
finely grated zest and juice of 1 lime

1 red chilli, deseeded and very finely
  chopped
1 tbsp soy sauce
¹/₂ tsp arrowroot
2 tbsp chopped fresh coriander
  (cilantro)
8 sheets filo pastry

25 g/1 oz butter
2 tsp sesame oil

TO SERVE:
chili sauce
spring onion (scallion) tassels

1 Using a sharp knife, cut the carrots into thin sticks. Deseed the (bell) pepper and cut into thin slices.

2 Heat the sunflower oil in a large preheated wok.

3 Add the carrot, red (bell) pepper and beansprouts and cook, stirring, for 2 minutes, or until softened. Remove the wok from the heat and toss in the lime zest and juice, and the red chilli.

4 Mix the soy sauce with the arrowroot. Stir the mixture into the wok, return to the heat and cook for 2 minutes or until the juices thicken. Add the coriander (cilantro) and mix well.

5 Lay the sheets of filo pastry out on a board. Melt the butter and sesame oil and brush each sheet with the mixture. Spoon a little of the vegetable filling at the top of each sheet, fold over each long side, and roll up.

6 Add a little oil to the wok and cook the spring rolls in batches, for 2–3 minutes, or until crisp and golden. Garnish with spring onion (scallion) tassels and serve hot with chilli dipping sauce.

COOK'S TIP

Use prepared spring roll skins available from Chinese supermarkets or health food shops instead of the filo pastry if liked.

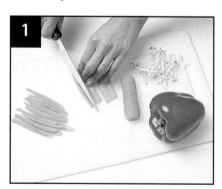

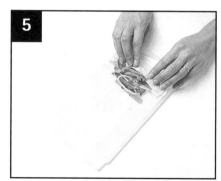

Seven Spice Aubergines (Eggplants)

*This is a really simple dish which is perfect
served with a chilli dip.*

Serves 4

INGREDIENTS

450 g/1 lb aubergines (eggplants),
  wiped
1 egg white

50 g/1^{3}/$_{4}$ oz/3^{1}/$_{2}$ tbsp cornflour
  (cornstarch)
1 tsp salt

1 tbsp Thai seven spice seasoning
oil, for deep-frying

1 Using a sharp knife, slice the aubergines (eggplants) into thin rings.

2 Place the egg white in a small bowl and whip until light and foamy.

3 Mix together the cornflour, salt and seven spice powder on a large plate.

4 Heat the oil for deep-frying in a large wok.

5 Dip each piece of aubergine (eggplant) into the beaten egg white then coat in the cornflour and seven spice mixture.

6 Deep-fry the coated aubergine (eggplant) slices, in batches, for 5 minutes, or until pale golden and crispy.

7 Transfer the aubergines (eggplants) to absorbent kitchen paper and leave to drain. Transfer to serving plates and serve hot.

COOK'S TIP

The best oil to use for deep-frying is groundnut oil which has a high smoke point and mild flavour, so it will neither burn or taint the food. About 600 ml/1 pint oil is sufficient.

COOK'S TIP

Thai seven spice seasoning can be found in the spice racks of most large supermarkets.

Stir-Fried Tofu (Bean Curd) with Peanut & Chilli Sauce

Golden pieces of tofu (bean curd) are served in a hot and creamy peanut sauce for a classic vegetarian starter.

Serves 4

INGREDIENTS

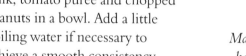

450 g/1 lb tofu (bean curd), cubed
oil, for frying

SAUCE:
6 tbsp crunchy peanut butter
1 tbsp sweet chilli sauce

150 ml/¹/₄ pint/²/₃ cup coconut milk
1 tbsp tomato purée
25 g/1 oz/¹/₄ cup chopped salted
  peanuts

1 Pat away any moisture from the tofu (bean curd), using absorbent kitchen paper.

2 Heat the oil in a large wok until very hot. Cook the tofu (bean curd), in batches, for about 5 minutes, or until golden and crispy. Remove the tofu (bean curd) with a slotted spoon, transfer to absorbent kitchen paper and leave to drain.

3 To make the sauce, mix together the crunchy peanut butter, sweet chilli sauce, coconut milk, tomato purée and chopped peanuts in a bowl. Add a little boiling water if necessary to achieve a smooth consistency.

4 Transfer the crispy fried tofu (bean curd) to serving plates and serve with the peanut and chilli sauce.

COOK'S TIP

Cook the peanut and chilli sauce in a saucepan over a gentle heat before serving, if you prefer.

COOK'S TIP

Make sure that all of the moisture has been absorbed from the tofu (bean curd) before frying, otherwise it will not crispen.

Crispy Seaweed

This is a tasty Chinese starter or accompaniment which is not all that it seems. Pak choi is fried, salted and tossed with pine kernels (nuts), seaweed being totally absent from the recipe!

Serves 4

INGREDIENTS

1 kg/2.4 lb pak choi
groundnut oil, for deep frying (about 850 ml/1$\frac{1}{2}$ pints/3$\frac{3}{4}$ cups)

1 tsp salt
1 tbsp caster (superfine) sugar

50 g/1$\frac{3}{4}$ oz/2$\frac{1}{2}$ tbsp toasted pine kernels (nuts)

1 Rinse the pak choi leaves under cold running water, then pat dry thoroughly with absorbent kitchen paper.

2 Roll each pak choi leaf up, then slice through thinly so that the leaves are finely shredded.

3 Heat the oil in a large wok. Carefully add the shredded leaves and fry for about 30 seconds or until they shrivel up and become crispy (you may need to do this in about 4 batches).

4 Remove the crispy seaweed from the wok with a slotted spoon and leave to drain on absorbent kitchen paper.

5 Transfer the crispy seaweed to a large bowl and toss with the salt, sugar and pine kernels (nuts). Serve immediately.

COOK'S TIP

As a time-saver you can use a food processor to shred the pak choi finely. Make sure you use only the best leaves; sort through the pak choi and discard any tough, outer leaves as these will spoil the overall taste and texture of the dish.

VARIATION

Use savoy cabbage instead of the pak choi if it is unavailable, making sure the leaves are well dried before frying.

Spicy Chicken Livers with Pak Choi

This is a richly flavoured dish with a dark, slightly tangy sauce which is popular in China.

Serves 4

INGREDIENTS

350 g/12 oz chicken livers
2 tbsp sunflower oil
1 red chilli, deseeded and finely chopped

1 tsp fresh grated ginger
2 cloves garlic, crushed
2 tbsp tomato ketchup
3 tbsp sherry

3 tbsp soy sauce
1 tsp cornflour (cornstarch)
450 g/1 lb pak choi
egg noodles, to serve

1 Using a sharp knife, trim the fat from the chicken livers and slice into small pieces.

2 Heat the oil in a large wok. Add the chicken liver pieces and stir-fry over a high heat for 2–3 minutes.

3 Add the chilli, ginger and garlic and stir-fry for about 1 minute.

4 Mix together the tomato ketchup, sherry, soy sauce and cornflour (cornstarch) in a small bowl and set aside.

5 Add the pak choi to the wok and stir-fry until it just wilts.

6 Add the reserved tomato ketchup mixture to the wok and cook, stirring to mix, until the juices start to bubble.

7 Transfer to serving bowls and serve hot with noodles.

COOK'S TIP

Fresh ginger root will keep for several weeks in a dry, cool place.

COOK'S TIP

Chicken livers are available fresh or frozen from most supermarkets.

Thai-style Fish Cakes

*These small fish cakes are quick to make
and are delicious served with a chilli dip.*

Serves 4

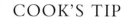
INGREDIENTS

450 g/1 lb cod fillets, skinned
2 tbsp fish sauce
2 red Thai chilies, deseeded and very
finely chopped

2 cloves garlic, crushed
10 lime leaves, very finely chopped
2 tbsp fresh coriander (cilantro),
chopped
1 large egg

25 g/1 oz/^{1}/$_4$ cup plain (all-purpose)
flour
100 g/3^1/$_2$ oz fine green beans, very
finely sliced
groundnut oil, for frying

1 Using a sharp knife, roughly cut the cod fillets into bite-sized pieces.

2 Place the cod pieces in a food processor together with the fish sauce, chillies, garlic, lime leaves, coriander (cilantro), egg and plain (all-purpose) flour. Process until finely chopped and turn out into a large mixing bowl.

3 Add the green beans to the cod mixture and combine.

4 Divide the mixture into small balls. Flatten the balls between the palms of your hands to form rounds.

5 Heat a little oil in a preheated wok. Fry the fish cakes on both sides until brown and crispy on the outside.

6 Transfer the fish cakes to serving plates and serve hot.

VARIATION

Almost any kind of fish fillets and seafood can used in this recipe, try haddock, crab meat or lobster.

COOK'S TIP

Fish sauce is a salty, brown liquid which is a must for authentic flavour. It is used to salt dishes but is milder in flavour than soy sauce. It is available from Asian food stores or health food shops.

Crispy Chilli & Peanut Prawns (Shrimp)

Peanut flavours are widely used in Far East and South East Asian cooking and complement many ingredients. Here, combined with fresh prawns (shrimp) they create a delicate and delicious dish.

Serves 4

INGREDIENTS

450 g/1 lb king prawns (peeled apart from tail end)
3 tbsp crunchy peanut butter

1 tbsp chilli sauce
10 sheets filo pastry
25 g/1 oz butter, melted

50 g/1³/₄ oz fine egg noodles
oil, for frying

1 Using a sharp knife, make a small horizontal slit across the back of each prawn (shrimp). Press down on the prawns (shrimps) so that they lie flat.

2 Mix together the peanut butter and chilli sauce in a small bowl. Spread a little of the sauce on to each prawn (shrimp).

3 Cut each pastry sheet in half and brush with melted butter.

4 Wrap each prawn (shrimp) in a piece of pastry, tucking the edges under to fully enclose the prawn (shrimp).

5 Place the egg noodles in a bowl, pour over enough boiling water to cover and leave to stand for 5 minutes. Drain the noodles thoroughly. Use 2–3 cooked noodles to tie around each prawn (shrimp).

6 Heat the oil in a preheated wok. Cook the prawns (shrimp) for 3–4 minutes, or until golden and crispy.

7 Remove the prawns (shrimp) with a slotted spoon, transfer to absorbent kitchen paper and leave to drain. Transfer to serving plates and serve warm.

COOK'S TIP

When using filo pastry, keep any unused pastry covered to prevent it drying out and becoming brittle.

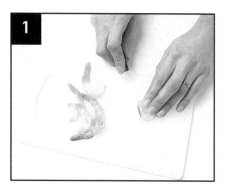

Prawn (Shrimp) Parcels

These small prawn (shrimp) bites are packed with the flavour of lime and coriander (cilantro) for a quick and tasty starter.

Serves 4

INGREDIENTS

1 tbsp sunflower oil
1 red (bell) pepper, deseeded and very
    thinly sliced
75 g/2³/₄ oz/³/₄ cup beansprouts
finely grated zest and juice of 1 lime
1 red Thai chili, deseeded and very
    finely chopped

1 cm/¹/₂ inch piece of root ginger,
    peeled and grated
225 g/8 oz peeled prawns (shrimp)
1 tbsp fish sauce
¹/₂ tsp arrowroot
2 tbsp chopped fresh coriander
    (cilantro)

8 sheets filo pastry
25 g/1 oz/2 tbsp butter
2 tsp sesame oil
oil, for frying
spring onion (scallion) tassels, to
    garnish
chilli sauce, to serve

1 Heat the sunflower oil in a large preheated wok. Add the red (bell) pepper and beansprouts and stir-fry for 2 minutes, or until the vegetables have softened.

2 Remove the wok from the heat and toss in the lime zest and juice, red chilli, ginger and prawns (shrimp), stirring well.

3 Mix the fish sauce with the arrowroot and stir the mixture into the wok juices.

Return the wok to the heat and cook, stirring, for 2 minutes, or until the juices thicken. Toss in the coriander (cilantro) and mix well.

4 Lay the sheets of filo pastry out on a board. Melt the butter and sesame oil and brush each pastry sheet with the mixture.

5 Spoon a little of the prawn (shrimp) filling on to the top of each sheet, fold over each end, and roll up to enclose the filling.

6 Heat the oil in a large wok. Cook the parcels, in batches, for 2–3 minutes, or until crisp and golden. Garnish with spring onion (scallion) tassels and serve hot with a chilli dipping sauce.

COOK'S TIP

If using cooked prawns (shrimp), cook for 1 minute only otherwise the prawns (shrimp) will toughen.

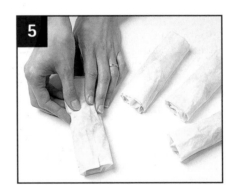

Chinese Prawn (Shrimp) Salad

Noodles and beansprouts form the basis of this refreshing salad which combines the flavours of fruit and prawns (shrimp) for a quick and delicious dish.

Serves 4

INGREDIENTS

250 g/9 oz fine egg noodles
3 tbsp sunflower oil
1 tbsp sesame oil
1 tbsp sesame seeds

150 g/5^{1}/$_{2}$ oz/1^{1}/$_{2}$ cups beansprouts
1 ripe mango, sliced
6 spring onions (scallions), sliced
75 g/2^{3}/$_{4}$ oz radish, sliced

350 g/12 oz peeled cooked prawns
(shrimp)
2 tbsp light soy sauce
1 tbsp sherry

1 Place the egg noodles in a large bowl and pour over enough boiling water to cover. Leave to stand for 10 minutes.

2 Drain the noodles thoroughly and pat away any moisture with absorbent kitchen paper.

3 Heat the sunflower oil in a large wok. Add the noodles and stir-fry for 5 minutes, tossing frequently.

4 Remove the wok from the heat and add the sesame oil, sesame seeds and beansprouts, tossing to mix well.

5 In a separate bowl, mix together the sliced mango, spring onions (scallions), radish, prawns (shrimp), light soy sauce and sherry.

6 Toss the prawn (shrimp) mixture with the noodles or alternatively, arrange the noodles around the edge of a serving plate and pile the prawn (shrimp) mixture into the centre. Serve immediately.

VARIATION

If fresh mango is unavailable, use canned mango slices, rinsed and drained, instead.

Sesame Prawn (Shrimp) Toasts

These are one of the most recognised and popular starters in Chinese restaurants in the Western world. Quick and easy to make they will soon feature on all of your dinner-party menus.

Serves 4

INGREDIENTS

4 slices medium, thick-sliced white bread
225 g/8 oz cooked peeled prawns (shrimp)

1 tbsp soy sauce
2 cloves garlic, crushed
1 tbsp sesame oil
1 egg

25 g/1 oz/2 tbsp sesame seeds
oil, for frying
sweet chilli sauce, to serve

1 Remove the crusts from the bread if desired, then set the slices of bread aside until required.

2 Place the peeled prawns (shrimp), soy sauce, crushed garlic, sesame oil and egg into a food processor and blend until a smooth paste has formed.

3 Spread the prawn (shrimp) paste evenly over the 4 slices of bread.

4 Sprinkle the sesame seeds over the top of the prawn (shrimp) mixture and press the seeds down with your hands so that they stick to the mixture.

5 Cut each slice in half and in half again to form 4 triangles.

6 Heat the oil in a large wok and deep-fry the toasts, sesame seed-side up, for 4-5 minutes, or until golden and crispy.

7 Remove the toasts with a slotted spoon and transfer to absorbent kitchen paper and leave to drain thoroughly.

8 Serve warm with sweet chilli sauce for dipping.

VARIATION

Add two chopped spring onions (scallions) to the mixture in step 2 for added flavour and crunch.

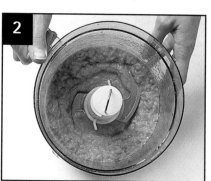

Prawn (Shrimp) Omelette

This is called Foo Yung *in China and is a classic dish which may be flavoured with any ingredients you have to hand. It is a quick and delicious omelette.*

Serves 4

INGREDIENTS

3 tbsp sunflower oil
2 leeks, trimmed and sliced
350 g/12 oz raw tiger prawns
   (shrimp)

25 g/1 oz/4 tbsp cornflour
   (cornstarch)
1 tsp salt
175 g/6 oz mushrooms, sliced

175 g/6 oz/1¹/₂ cups beansprouts
6 eggs
deep-fried leeks, to garnish (optional)

1 Heat the sunflower oil in a preheated wok. Add the leeks and stir-fry for 3 minutes.

2 Rinse the prawns (shrimp) under cold running water and then pat dry with absorbent kitchen paper.

3 Mix together the cornflour (cornstarch) and salt in a large bowl.

4 Add the prawns (shrimp) to the cornflour (cornstarch) and salt mixture and toss to coat all over.

5 Add the prawns (shrimp) to the wok and stir-fry for 2 minutes, or until the prawns (shrimp) are almost cooked through.

6 Add the mushrooms and beansprouts to the wok and stir-fry for a further 2 minutes.

7 Beat the eggs with 3 tablespoons of cold water. Pour the egg mixture into the wok and cook until the egg sets, carefully turning over once. Turn the omelette out on to a clean board, divide into 4 and serve hot,

garnished with deep-fried leeks (if using).

COOK'S TIP

If liked, divide the mixture into 4 once the initial cooking has taken place in step 6 and cook 4 individual omelettes.

Salt & Pepper Prawns (Shrimp)

Szechuan peppercorns are very hot, adding heat and a red colour to the prawns (shrimp).
They are effectively offset by the sugar in this recipe.

Serves 4

INGREDIENTS

2 tsp salt
1 tsp black pepper
2 tsp Szechuan peppercorns
1 tsp sugar

450 g/1 lb peeled raw tiger prawns (shrimp)
2 tbsp groundnut oil
1 red chilli, deseeded and finely chopped

1 tsp freshly grated ginger
3 cloves garlic, crushed
spring onions (scallions), sliced, to garnish
prawn (shrimp) crackers, to serve

1 Grind the salt, black pepper and Szechuan peppercorns in a pestle and mortar. Mix the salt and pepper mixture with the sugar and set aside until required.

2 Rinse the prawns (shrimp) under cold running water and pat dry with absorbent kitchen paper.

3 Heat the oil in a preheated wok. Add the prawns (shrimp), chilli, ginger and garlic and stir-fry for 4–5 minutes, or until the prawns (shrimp) are cooked through.

4 Add the salt and pepper mixture to the wok and stir-fry for 1 minute.

5 Transfer to warm serving bowls and garnish with spring onions (scallion). Serve hot with prawn (shrimp) crackers.

COOK'S TIP

Szechuan peppercorns are also known as farchiew. *These wild reddish-brown peppercorns from the Szechuan region of China add an aromatic flavour to a dish.*

COOK'S TIP

Tiger prawns (shrimps) are widely available and are not only colourful and tasty, but they have a meaty texture, too. If cooked tiger prawns (shrimp) are used, add them with the salt and pepper mixture in step 4 – if the cooked prawns (shrimp) are added any earlier they will toughen up and be inedible.

Meat & Poultry

Meat is expensive in Far Eastern countries and is eaten in smaller proportions than in the Western world. However, meat is used to its full potential – it is marinated or spiced and combined with other delicious native flavourings to create a wide array of delicious dishes.

In Malaysia, a wide variety of spicy meats is offered, reflecting the many ethnic origins of the population. Chicken is the most frequently used poultry in Malaysia – it is marinated, grilled and stir-fried or cooked in the wok as delicious curries and stews.

In China, poultry, lamb, beef and pork are stir-fried or steamed in the wok and combined with sauces and seasonings such as soy, black bean and oyster sauce, and in Japan where a smaller amount of meat is consumed, it is generally marinated and quickly stir-fried in a wok or simmered in miso stock.

The use of meat in Thailand is similar, but it is leaner and has more flavour due to 'free-range' rearing. Meats differ slightly in that beef is probably taken from the buffalo, and lamb on the menu can often turn out to be goat! There are no such demands in the following chapter, commonly available meats are perfectly acceptable.

Stir-Fried Ginger Chicken

The oranges add colour and piquancy to this refreshing dish,
which complements the chicken well.

Serves 4

INGREDIENTS

2 tbsp sunflower oil
1 onion, sliced
175 g/6 oz carrots, cut into thin
  sticks
1 clove garlic, crushed

350 g/12 oz boneless skinless chicken
  breasts
2 tbsp fresh ginger, peeled and
  grated
1 tsp ground ginger
4 tbsp sweet sherry

1 tbsp tomato purée
1 tbsp demerara sugar
100 ml/3^1/2 fl oz/^{1}/3 cup orange juice
1 tsp cornflour (cornstarch)
1 orange, peeled and segmented
fresh snipped chives, to garnish

1 Heat the oil in a large preheated wok. Add the onion, carrots and garlic and stir-fry over a high heat for 3 minutes or until the vegetables begin to soften.

2 Using a sharp knife, slice the chicken into thin strips. Add the chicken to the wok together with the fresh ginger and ground ginger. Stir-fry for a further 10 minutes, or until the chicken is well cooked through and golden in colour.

3 Mix together the sherry, tomato purée, sugar, orange juice and cornflour (cornstarch) in a bowl. Stir the mixture into the wok and heat through until the mixture bubbles and the juices start to thicken.

4 Add the orange segments and carefully toss to mix.

5 Transfer the stir-fried chicken to warm serving bowls and garnish with freshly snipped chives. Serve immediately.

COOK'S TIP

Make sure that you do not continue cooking the dish once the orange segments have been added in step 4, otherwise they will break up.

Chicken, Spring Green & Yellow Bean Stir-Fry

Yellow bean sauce is made from yellow soy beans and is available in most supermarkets. Try to buy a chunky sauce rather than a smooth sauce for texture.

Serves 4

INGREDIENTS

2 tbsp sunflower oil
450 g/1 lb skinless, boneless chicken breasts
2 cloves garlic, crushed

1 green (bell) pepper
100 g/3^1/$_2$ oz/1^1/$_2$ cups mangetout (snow peas)
6 spring onions (scallions), sliced, plus extra to garnish

225 g/8 oz spring greens or cabbage, shredded
160 g/5^3/$_4$ oz jar yellow bean sauce
50 g/1^3/$_4$ oz/3 tbsp roasted cashew nuts

1 Heat the sunflower oil in a large preheated wok.

2 Using a sharp knife, slice the chicken into thin strips.

3 Add the chicken to the wok together with the garlic. Stir-fry for about 5 minutes or until the chicken is sealed on all sides and beginning to turn golden.

4 Using a sharp knife, deseed the green (bell) pepper and cut into thin strips.

5 Add the mangetout (snow peas), spring onions (scallions), green (bell) pepper strips and spring greens or cabbage to the wok. Stir-fry for a further 5 minutes or until the vegetables are just tender.

6 Stir in the yellow bean sauce and heat through for about 2 minutes or until the mixture starts to bubble.

7 Scatter with the roasted cashew nuts.

8 Transfer the chicken, spring green and yellow bean stir-fry to warm serving plates and garnish with extra spring onions (scallions), if desired. Serve the stir-fry immediately.

COOK'S TIP

Do not add salted cashew nuts to this dish otherwise, combined with the slightly salty sauce, the dish will be very salty indeed.

Chicken, (Bell) Pepper & Orange Stir-Fry

Chicken thighs are inexpensive, meaty portions of the chicken which are readily available.
The meat is not as tender as the breast but it is perfect for stir-frying.

Serves 4

INGREDIENTS

3 tbsp sunflower oil
350 g/12 oz boneless chicken thighs,
   skinned and cut into thin strips
1 onion, sliced
1 clove garlic, crushed

1 red (bell) pepper, deseeded and
   sliced
75 g/2³/4 oz/1¹/4 cups mangetout
   (snow peas)
4 tbsp light soy sauce
4 tbsp sherry

1 tbsp tomato purée
finely grated rind and juice of 1 orange
1 tsp cornflour (cornstarch)
2 oranges
100 g/3¹/2 oz/1 cup beansprouts
cooked rice or noodles, to serve

1 Heat the sunflower oil in a large preheated wok.

2 Add the strips of chicken to the wok and stir-fry for 2–3 minutes or until sealed on all sides.

3 Add the sliced onion, garlic, (bell) pepper and mangetout (snow peas) to the wok. Stir-fry the mixture for a further 5 minutes, or until the vegetables are just becoming tender and the chicken is completely cooked through.

4 Mix together the soy sauce, sherry, tomato purée, orange rind and juice and the cornflour (cornstarch) in a measuring jug.

5 Add the mixture to the wok and cook, stirring, until the juices start to thicken.

6 Using a sharp knife, peel and segment the oranges.

7 Add the orange segments and beansprouts to the mixture in the wok and heat through for a further 2 minutes.

8 Transfer the stir-fry to serving plates and serve at once with cooked rice or noodles.

COOK'S TIP

Beansprouts are sprouting mung beans and are a regular ingredient in Chinese cooking. They require very little cooking and may even be eaten raw, if wished.

Coconut Chicken Curry

Okra or ladies fingers are slightly bitter in flavour. The pineapple and coconut in this recipe offsets them in both colour and flavour.

Serves 4

INGREDIENTS

2 tbsp sunflower oil or 25 g/1 oz ghee

450 g/1 lb boneless, skinless chicken thighs or breasts

150 g/5^1/2 oz/1 cup okra

1 large onion, sliced

2 cloves garlic, crushed

3 tbsp mild curry paste

300 ml/^{1}/2 pint/2^1/4 cups chicken stock

1 tbsp fresh lemon juice

100 g/3^1/2 oz/^{1}/2 cup creamed coconut

175 g/6 oz/1^1/4 cups fresh or canned pineapple, cubed

150 ml/^{1}/4 pint/^{2}/3 cup thick, natural yogurt

2 tbsp chopped fresh coriander (cilantro)

freshly boiled rice, to serve

TO GARNISH:

lemon wedges

fresh coriander (cilantro) sprigs

1 Heat the sunflower oil or ghee in a large preheated wok.

2 Using a sharp knife, cut the chicken into bite-sized pieces. Add the chicken to the wok and cook, stirring frequently, until evenly browned.

3 Using a sharp knife, trim the okra.

4 Add the onion, garlic and okra to the wok and cook

for a further 2–3 minutes, stirring constantly.

5 Mix the curry paste with the chicken stock and lemon juice and pour over the mixture in the wok. Bring to the boil, cover and leave to simmer for 30 minutes.

6 Coarsley grate the creamed coconut, stir it into the curry and cook for about 5 minutes – the creamed coconut will help to thicken the juices.

7 Add the pineapple, yogurt and coriander (cilantro) and heat through for 2 minutes, stirring.

8 Garnish and serve hot with boiled rice.

COOK'S TIP

Score around the top of the okra with a knife before cooking to release the sticky glue-like substance which is bitter in taste.

Sweet & Sour Chicken with Mango

This is quite a sweet dish as mango has a sweet, scented flavour.

Serves 4

INGREDIENTS

1 tbsp sunflower oil
6 skinless, boneless chicken thighs
1 ripe mango
2 cloves garlic, crushed

225 g/8 oz leeks, shredded
100 g/3^1/$_2$ oz/1 cup beansprouts
150 ml/^{1}/$_4$ pint/^{2}/$_3$ cup mango juice
1 tbsp white wine vinegar

2 tbsp clear honey
2 tbsp tomato ketchup
1 tsp cornflour (cornstarch)

1 Heat the sunflower oil in a large preheated wok.

2 Using a sharp knife, cut the chicken into bite-sized cubes.

3 Add the chicken to the wok and stir-fry over a high heat for 10 minutes, tossing frequently until the chicken is cooked through and golden in colour.

4 Meanwhile, peel and slice the mango.

5 Add the garlic, leeks, mango and beansprouts to the wok and stir-fry for a further 2–3 minutes, or until softened.

6 Mix together the mango juice, white wine vinegar, clear honey and tomato ketchup with the cornflour (cornstarch) in a measuring jug.

7 Pour the mango juice and cornflour (cornstarch) mixture into the wok and stir-fry for a further 2 minutes, or until the juices start to thicken.

8 Transfer to a warmed serving dish and serve immediately.

COOK'S TIP

Mango juice is avaialable in jars from most supermarkets and is quite thick and sweet. If unavailable, purée and sieve a ripe mango and add a little water to make up the required quantity.

Chicken Stir-Fry with Cumin Seeds & Trio of (Bell) Peppers

Cumin seeds are more frequently associated with Indian cooking, but they are used in this Chinese recipe for their earthy flavour. You could use ¹/₂ tsp of ground cumin instead.

Serves 4

INGREDIENTS

450 g/1 lb boneless, skinless chicken breasts
2 tbsp sunflower oil
1 clove garlic, crushed
1 tbsp cumin seeds
1 tbsp grated fresh ginger root

1 red chilli, deseeded and sliced
1 red (bell) pepper, deseeded and sliced
1 green (bell) pepper, deseeded and sliced
1 yellow (bell) pepper, deseeded and sliced

100 g/3¹/₂ oz/1 cup beansprouts
350 g/12 oz pak choi or other green leaves
2 tbsp sweet chilli sauce
3 tbsp light soy sauce
deep-fried crispy ginger, to garnish (see Cook's Tip)

1 Using a sharp knife, slice the chicken breasts into thin strips.

2 Heat the oil in a large preheated wok.

3 Add the chicken to the wok and stir-fry for 5 minutes.

4 Add the garlic, cumin seeds, ginger and chilli to the wok, stirring to mix.

5 Add all of the (bell) peppers to the wok and stir-fry for a further 5 minutes.

6 Toss in the beansprouts and pak choi together with the sweet chilli sauce and soy sauce and continue to cook until the pak choi leaves start to wilt.

7 Transfer to warm serving bowls and garnish with deep-fried ginger (see Cook's Tip).

COOK'S TIP

To make the deep-fried ginger garnish, peel and thinly slice a large piece of root ginger, using a sharp knife. Carefully lower the slices of ginger into a wok or small pan of hot oil and cook for about 30 seconds. Remove the deep-fried ginger with a slotted spoon, transfer to sheets of absorbent kitchen paper and leave to drain thoroughly.

Stir-Fried Chicken with Lemon & Sesame Seeds

Sesame seeds have a strong flavour which adds nuttiness to recipes.
They are perfect for coating these thin chicken strips.

Serves 4

INGREDIENTS

4 boneless, skinless chicken breasts
1 egg white
25 g/1 oz/2 tbsp sesame seeds
2 tbsp vegetable oil

1 onion, sliced
1 tbsp demerara sugar
finely grated zest and juice of
  1 lemon

3 tbsp lemon curd
200 g/7 oz can waterchestnuts
lemon zest, to garnish

1 Place the chicken breasts between 2 sheets of cling film (plastic wrap) and pound with a rolling pin to flatten. Slice the chicken into thin strips.

2 Whisk the egg white until light and foamy.

3 Dip the chicken strips into the egg white, then into the sesame seeds until coated evenly.

4 Heat the oil in a large preheated wok.

5 Add the onion to the wok and stir-fry for 2 minutes or until just softened.

6 Add the sesame-coated chicken to the wok and continue stir-frying for 5 minutes, or until the chicken turns golden.

7 Mix together the sugar, lemon zest, lemon juice and the lemon curd and add the mixture to the wok. Allow the lemon mixture to bubble slightly without stirring.

8 Drain the waterchestnuts and slice them thinly, using a sharp knife. Add the waterchestnuts to the wok and heat through for 2 minutes. Transfer to serving bowls, garnish with lemon zest and serve hot.

COOK'S TIP

Waterchestnuts are commonly added to Chinese recipes for their crunchy texture as they do not have a great deal of flavour.

Thai Red Chicken with Cherry Tomatoes

This is a really colourful dish, the red of the tomatoes perfectly complementing the orange sweet potato.

Serves 4

INGREDIENTS

1 tbsp sunflower oil
450 g/1 lb boneless, skinless chicken
2 cloves garlic, crushed
2 tbsp Thai red curry paste
2 tbsp fresh grated galangal or root
  ginger

1 tbsp tamarind paste
4 lime leaves
225 g/8 oz sweet potato
600 ml/1 pint/2^1/2 cups coconut milk
225 g/8 oz cherry tomatoes, halved

3 tbsp chopped fresh coriander
  (cilantro)
cooked jasmine or Thai fragrant rice,
  to serve

1 Heat the sunflower oil in a large preheated wok.

2 Thinly slice the chicken. Add the chicken to the wok and stir-fry for 5 minutes.

3 Add the garlic, curry paste, galangal or root ginger, tamarind and lime leaves to the wok and stir-fry for 1 minute.

4 Using a sharp knife, peel and dice the sweet potato.

5 Add the coconut milk and sweet potato to the mixture in the wok and bring to the boil. Allow to bubble over a medium heat for 20 minutes, or until the juices start to thicken and reduce.

6 Add the cherry tomatoes and coriander (cilantro) to the curry and cook for a further 5 minutes, stirring occasionally. Transfer to serving plates and serve hot with cooked jasmine or Thai fragrant rice.

COOK'S TIP

Galangal is a spice very similar to ginger and is used to replace the latter in Thai cuisine. It can be bought fresh from Oriental food stores but is also available dried and as a powder. The fresh root, which is not as pungent as ginger, needs to be peeled before slicing to use.

Peppered Chicken Stir-fried with Sugar Snap Peas

Crushed mixed peppercorns coat tender, thin strips of chicken which are cooked with green and red (bell) peppers for a really colourful dish.

Serves 4

INGREDIENTS

2 tbsp tomato ketchup
2 tbsp soy sauce
450 g/1 lb boneless, skinless chicken
    breasts

2 tbsp crushed mixed peppercorns
2 tbsp sunflower oil
1 red (bell) pepper
1 green (bell) pepper

175 g/6 oz/2^1/$_2$ cups sugar snap peas
2 tbsp oyster sauce

1 Mix the tomato ketchup with the soy sauce in a bowl.

2 Using a sharp knife, slice the chicken into thin strips. Toss the chicken in the tomato ketchup and soy sauce mixture.

3 Sprinkle the crushed peppercorns on to a plate. Dip the coated chicken in the peppercorns until evenly coated.

4 Heat the sunflower oil in a preheated wok.

5 Add the chicken to the wok and stir-fry for 5 minutes.

6 Deseed and slice the (bell) peppers.

7 Add the (bell) peppers to the wok together with the sugar snap peas and stir-fry for a further 5 minutes.

8 Add the oyster sauce and allow to bubble for 2 minutes. Transfer to serving bowls and serve immediately.

VARIATION

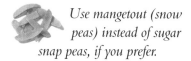

Use mangetout (snow peas) instead of sugar snap peas, if you prefer.

Honey & Soy Stir-Fried Chicken with Beansprouts

Clear honey is often added to Chinese recipes for sweetness.
It combines well with the saltiness of the soy sauce.

Serves 4

INGREDIENTS

2 tbsp clear honey
3 tbsp light soy sauce
1 tsp Chinese five spice powder
1 tbsp sweet sherry
1 clove garlic, crushed

8 chicken thighs
1 tbsp sunflower oil
1 red chilli

100 g/3$^{1}/_{2}$ oz/1$^{1}/_{4}$ cups baby corn
  cobs, halved
8 spring onions (scallions), sliced
150 g/5$^{1}/_{2}$ oz/1$^{1}/_{2}$ cups beansprouts

1 Mix together the honey, soy sauce, Chinese five spice powder, sherry and garlic in a large bowl.

2 Using a sharp knife, make 3 slashes in the skin of each chicken thigh. Brush the honey and soy marinade over the chicken thighs, cover and leave to stand for at least 30 minutes.

3 Heat the oil in a large preheated wok.

4 Add the chicken to the wok and cook over a fairly high heat for 12–15 minutes, or until the chicken browns and the skin begins to crispen. Remove the chicken with a slotted spoon.

5 Using a sharp knife, deseed and very finely chop the chilli.

6 Add the chilli, corn cobs, spring onions (scallions) and beansprouts to the wok and stir-fry for 5 minutes.

7 Return the chicken to the wok and mix all of the ingredients together until completely heated through.

8 Transfer to serving plates and serve immediately.

COOK'S TIP

Chinese five spice powder is found in most large supermarkets and is a blend of aromatic spices.

Stir-Fried Chicken with Cashew Nuts & Yellow Bean Sauce

Chicken and cashew nuts are a great classic combination, and this recipe is no exception.
Flavoured with yellow bean sauce it is a quick and delicious dish.

Serves 4

INGREDIENTS

450 g/1 lb boneless chicken breasts
2 tbsp vegetable oil
1 red onion, sliced

175 g/6 oz/1^1/$_2$ cups flat mushrooms, sliced
100 g/3^1/$_2$ oz/^{1}/$_3$ cup cashew nuts

75 g/2^3/$_4$ oz jar yellow bean sauce
fresh coriander (cilantro), to garnish
egg fried rice or plain boiled rice,
   to serve

1 Using a sharp knife, remove the excess skin from the chicken breasts if desired. Cut the chicken into small, bite-sized chunks.

2 Heat the vegetable oil in a preheated wok.

3 Add the chicken to the wok and stir-fry for 5 minutes.

4 Add the red onion and mushrooms to the wok and continue to stir-fry for a further 5 minutes.

5 Place the cashew nuts on a baking tray (cookie sheet) and toast under a preheated medium grill (broiler) until just browning – this brings out their flavour.

6 Toss the toasted cashew nuts into the wok together with the yellow bean sauce. Allow the sauce to bubble for 2–3 minutes.

7 Transfer to warm serving bowls and garnish with fresh coriander (cilantro). Serve hot with egg fried rice or plain boiled rice.

COOK'S TIP

Chicken thighs could be used instead of the chicken breasts for a more economical dish.

Stir-Fried Chicken with Chilli & Crispy Basil

Chicken drumsticks are cooked in a delicious sauce and served with deep-fried basil for colour and flavour.

Serves 4

INGREDIENTS

8 chicken drumsticks
2 tbsp soy sauce
1 tbsp sunflower oil
1 red chilli

100 g/3¹/₂ oz carrots, cut into thin sticks
6 celery stalks, cut into sticks
3 tbsp sweet chilli sauce

oil, for frying
about 50 fresh basil leaves

1 Remove the skin from the chicken drumsticks if desired. Make 3 slashes in each drumstick. Brush the drumsticks with the soy sauce.

2 Heat the oil in a preheated wok and fry the drumsticks for 20 minutes, turning frequently, until they are cooked through.

3 Deseed and finely chop the chilli. Add the chilli, carrots and celery to the wok and cook for a further 5 minutes. Stir in the chilli sauce, cover and allow to bubble gently whilst preparing the basil leaves.

4 Heat a little oil in a heavy based pan. Carefully add the basil leaves – stand well away from the pan and protect your hand with a tea towel (dish cloth) as they may spit a little. Cook for about 30 seconds or until they begin to curl up but not brown. Transfer to kitchen paper to drain.

5 Arrange the cooked chicken, vegetables and pan juices on to a warm serving plate and garnish with the deep-fried crispy basil leaves.

COOK'S TIP

Basil has a very strong flavour which is perfect with chicken and Chinese flavourings. You could use baby spinach instead of the basil, if you prefer.

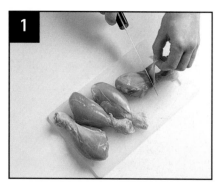

Stir-Fried Garlic Chicken with Coriander (Cilantro) & Lime

Garlic and coriander (cilantro) butter flavours and moistens chicken breasts which are served with a caramelised sauce, sharpened with lime juice.

Serves 4

INGREDIENTS

4 large skinless, boneless chicken breasts
50 g/1³/₄ oz/3 tbsp garlic butter, softened

3 tbsp chopped fresh coriander (cilantro)
1 tbsp sunflower oil
finely grated zest and juice of 2 limes

25 g/1 oz/4 tbsp palm sugar or demerara sugar
boiled rice, to serve

1 Place each chicken breast between 2 sheets of cling film (plastic wrap) and pound with a rolling pin until flattened to about 1 cm/¹/₂ inch thick.

2 Mix together the garlic butter and coriander (cilantro) and spread over each flattened chicken breast. Roll up like a Swiss roll and secure with a cocktail stick.

3 Heat the oil in a wok. Add the chicken rolls and cook, turning, for 15–20 minutes or until cooked through.

4 Remove the chicken from the wok and transfer to a board. Cut each chicken roll into slices.

5 Add the lime zest, juice and sugar to the wok and heat gently, stirring, until the sugar has dissolved. Raise the heat and allow to bubble for 2 minutes.

6 Arrange the chicken on warmed serving plates and spoon the pan juices over to serve.

7 Garnish with extra coriander (cilantro) if desired

COOK'S TIP

Be sure to check that the chicken is cooked through before slicing and serving. Cook over a gentle heat so as not to overcook the outside, while the inside remains raw.

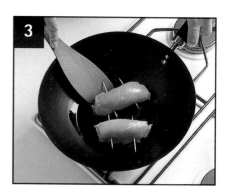

Stir-Fried Chicken with Cumin Seeds & Aubergine (Eggplant)

This is a delicious curried chicken and aubergine (eggplant) dish, flavoured with tomatoes and seasoned with fresh mint.

Serves 4

INGREDIENTS

5 tbsp sunflower oil
2 cloves garlic, crushed
1 tbsp cumin seeds
1 tbsp mild curry powder
1 tbsp paprika

450 g/1 lb boneless, skinless chicken breasts
1 large aubergine (eggplant), cubed
4 tomatoes, cut into quarters
100 ml/3$\frac{1}{2}$ fl oz/$\frac{1}{3}$ cup chicken stock

1 tbsp fresh lemon juice
$\frac{1}{2}$ tsp salt
150 ml/$\frac{1}{4}$ pint/$\frac{2}{3}$ cup natural yogurt
1 tbsp chopped fresh mint

1 Heat 2 tablespoons of the sunflower oil in a large preheated wok.

2 Add the garlic, cumin seeds, curry powder and paprika to the wok and stir-fry for 1 minute.

3 Using a sharp knife, thinly slice the chicken breasts.

4 Add the rest of the oil to the wok and stir-fry the chicken for 5 minutes.

5 Add the aubergine (eggplant) cubes, tomatoes and chicken stock and bring to the boil. Reduce the heat and leave to simmer for about 20 minutes.

6 Stir in the lemon juice, salt and yogurt and cook over a gentle heat for a further 5 minutes, stirring occasionally.

7 Scatter with chopped fresh mint and transfer to serving bowls. Serve immediately.

COOK'S TIP

Once the yogurt has been added, do not boil the sauce as the yogurt will curdle.

Hoisin Duck with Leek & Stir-Fried Cabbage

Duck is a strongly-flavoured meat which benefits from the added citrus peel to counteract this rich taste.

Serves 4

INGREDIENTS

4 duck breasts
350 g/12 oz green cabbage, thinly shredded

225 g/8 oz leeks, sliced
finely grated zest of 1 orange
6 tbsp oyster sauce

1 tsp toasted sesame seeds, to serve

1 Heat a large wok and dry-fry the duck breasts, with the skin on, for 5 minutes on each side (you may need to do this in 2 batches).

2 Remove the duck breasts from the wok and transfer to a clean board. Using a sharp knife, cut the duck breasts into thin slices.

3 Remove all but 1 tablespoon of the fat from the duck left in the wok; discard the rest.

4 Using a sharp knife, thinly shred the green cabbage.

5 Add the leeks, green cabbage and orange zest to the wok and stir-fry for 5 minutes, or until the vegetables have softened.

6 Return the duck to the wok and heat through for 2–3 minutes.

7 Drizzle the oyster sauce over the top of the duck, toss well to combine and then heat through.

8 Scatter with toasted sesame seeds and serve hot.

VARIATION

Use Chinese leaves for a lighter, sweeter flavour instead of the green cabbage, if you prefer.

Duck with Baby Corn Cobs & Pineapple

*The pineapple and plum sauce add a sweetness and fruity flavour
to this colourful recipe which blend well with the duck.*

Serves 4

INGREDIENTS

4 duck breasts
1 tsp Chinese five spice powder
1 tbsp cornflour (cornstarch)
1 tbsp chilli oil

225 g/8 oz baby onions, peeled
2 cloves garlic, crushed
100 g/3^1/$_2$ oz/1 cup baby corn cobs
175 g/6 oz/1^1/$_4$ cups canned
 pineapple chunks

6 spring onions (scallions), sliced
100 g/3^1/$_2$ oz/1 cup beansprouts
2 tbsp plum sauce

1 Remove any skin from the duck breasts. Cut the duck breasts into thin slices.

2 Mix together the five spice powder and the cornflour (cornstarch) in a large bowl.

3 Toss the duck in the five spice powder and cornflour (cornstarch) mixture until well coated.

4 Heat the oil in a preheated wok. Stir-fry the duck for 10 minutes, or until just begining to crispen around the edges.

5 Remove the duck from the wok and set aside until required.

6 Add the onions and garlic to the wok and stir-fry for 5 minutes, or until the onions have softened.

7 Add the baby corn cobs to the wok and stir-fry for a further 5 minutes.

8 Add the pineapple, spring onions (scallions) and beansprouts and stir-fry for 3–4 minutes. Stir in the plum sauce.

9 Return the cooked duck to the wok and toss until well mixed. Transfer to warm serving dishes and serve hot.

COOK'S TIP

Buy pineapple chunks in natural juice rather than syrup for a fresher flavour. If you can only obtain pineapple in syrup, rinse it in cold water and drain thoroughly before using.

Stir-Fried Turkey with Cranberry Glaze

This dish encompasses all of the flavours of Christmas with a Chinese theme! Turkey, cranberries, ginger, chestnuts and soy sauce all blend perfectly in this quick stir-fry.

Serves 2–3

INGREDIENTS

1 turkey breast
2 tbsp sunflower oil
15 g/^{1}/$_2$ oz/2 tbsp stem ginger

50 g/1^3/$_4$ oz/^{1}/$_2$ cup fresh or frozen cranberries
100 g/3^1/$_2$ oz/^{1}/$_4$ cup canned chestnuts

4 tbsp cranberry sauce
3 tbsp light soy sauce
salt and pepper

1 Remove any skin from the turkey breast. Using a sharp knife, thinly slice the turkey breast.

2 Heat the oil in a large preheated wok.

3 Add the turkey to the wok and stir-fry for 5 minutes, or until cooked through.

4 Using a sharp knife, finely chop the stem ginger.

5 Add the ginger and the cranberries to the wok and stir-fry for 2–3 minutes or until the cranberries have softened.

6 Add the chestnuts, cranberry sauce and soy sauce, season to taste with salt and pepper and allow to bubble for 2–3 minutes.

7 Transfer to warm serving dishes and serve immediately.

COOK'S TIP

If you wish, use a turkey escalope instead of the breast for really tender, lean meat.

COOK'S TIP

It is very important that the wok is very hot before you stir-fry. Test by by holding your hand flat about 7.5 cm/3 inches above the base of the interior – you should be able to feel the heat radiating from it.

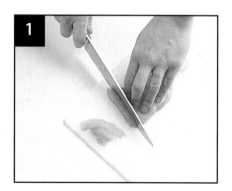

Stir-Fried Beef & Vegetables with Sherry & Soy Sauce

Fillet of beef is perfect for stir-frying as it is so tender and lends itself to quick cooking.

Serves 4

INGREDIENTS

2 tbsp sunflower oil
350 g/12 oz fillet of beef, sliced
1 red onion, sliced
175 g/6 oz courgettes (zucchini), sliced diagonally
175 g/6 oz carrots, thinly sliced
1 red (bell) pepper, deseeded and sliced

1 small head Chinese leaves, shredded
150 g/5^1/$_2$ oz/1^1/$_2$ cups beansprouts
225 g/8 oz can bamboo shoots, drained
150 g/5^1/$_2$ oz/^{1}/$_2$ cup cashew nuts, toasted

SAUCE:
3 tbsp medium sherry
3 tbsp light soy sauce
1 tsp ground ginger
1 clove garlic, crushed
1 tsp cornflour (cornstarch)
1 tbsp tomato purée

1 Heat the sunflower oil in a large preheated wok.

2 Add the beef and onion to the wok and stir-fry for 4–5 minutes or until the onion begins to soften and the meat is just browning.

3 Using a sharp knife, trim the courgette (zucchini) and slice diagonally.

4 Add the carrots, (bell) pepper, and courgettes (zucchini) and stir-fry for 5 minutes.

5 Toss in the Chinese leaves, beansprouts and bamboo shoots and heat through for 2–3 minutes, or until the leaves are just beginning to wilt.

6 Scatter the cashews nuts over the stir-fry.

7 To make the sauce, mix together the sherry, soy sauce, ground ginger, garlic, cornflour (cornstarch) and tomato purée. Pour the sauce over the stir-fry and toss until well combined. Allow the sauce to bubble for 2–3 minutes or until the juices start to thicken.

8 Transfer to warm serving dishes and serve at once.

Chilli Beef Stir-Fry Salad

This dish has a Mexican feel to it, combining all of the classic flavours.

Serves 4

INGREDIENTS

450 g/1 lb lean rump steak
2 cloves garlic, crushed
1 tsp chilli powder
$\frac{1}{2}$ tsp salt
1 tsp ground coriander

1 ripe avocado
30 ml/2 tbsp sunflower oil
425 g/15 oz can red kidney beans, drained
175 g/6 oz cherry tomatoes, halved

1 large packet tortilla chips
shredded iceberg lettuce
chopped fresh coriander (cilantro), to serve

1 Using a sharp knife, slice the beef into thin strips.

2 Place the garlic, chilli powder, salt and ground coriander in a large bowl and mix until well combined.

3 Add the strips of beef to the marinade and toss well to coat all over.

4 Using a sharp knife, peel the avocado. Slice the avocado lengthways and then crossways to form small dice.

5 Heat the oil in a large preheated wok. Add the beef and stir-fry for 5 minutes, tossing frequently.

6 Add the kidney beans, tomatoes and avocado and heat through for 2 minutes.

7 Arrange a bed of tortilla chips and iceberg lettuce around the edge of a large serving plate and spoon the beef mixture into the centre. Alternatively, serve the tortilla chips and iceberg lettuce separately.

8 Garnish with chopped fresh coriander (cilantro) and serve immediately.

COOK'S TIP

Serve this dish immediately as avocado tends to discolour quickly. Once you have cut the avocado into dice, sprinkle it with a little lemon juice to prevent discoloration.

Marinated Beef Stir-Fry with Bamboo Shoots & Mangetout (Snow Peas)

Tender beef, marinated in a soy and tomato sauce, is quickly stir-fried with crisp bamboo shoots and mangetout (snow peas) in this simple recipe.

Serves 4

INGREDIENTS

350 g/12 oz rump steak
3 tbsp dark soy sauce
1 tbsp tomato ketchup
2 cloves garlic, crushed

1 tbsp fresh lemon juice
1 tsp ground coriander
2 tbsp vegetable oil

175 g/6 oz/2³/4 cups mangetout
  (snow peas)
200 g/7 oz can bamboo shoots
1 tsp sesame oil

1 Using a sharp knife, thinly slice the meat.

2 Place the meat in a non metallic dish together with the dark soy sauce, tomato ketchup, garlic, lemon juice and ground coriander. Mix well so that all of the meat is coated in the marinade, cover and leave for at least 1 hour.

3 Heat the vegetable oil in a preheated wok. Add the meat to the wok and stir-fry for

2–4 minutes (depending on how well cooked you like your meat) or until cooked through.

4 Add the mangetout (snow peas) and bamboo shoots to the mixture in the wok and stir-fry over a high heat, tossing frequently, for a further 5 minutes.

5 Drizzle with the sesame oil and toss well to combine.

6 Transfer to serving dishes and serve hot.

COOK'S TIP

Leave the meat to marinate for at least 1 hour in order for the flavour to penetrate and increase the tenderness of the meat. If possible, leave for a little longer for a fuller flavour to develop.

Stir-Fried Beef with Baby Onions & Palm Sugar

*Palm sugar or brown sugar is used in this recipe to give the beef
a slightly caramelised flavour.*

Serves 4

INGREDIENTS

450 g/1 lb fillet beef
2 tbsp soy sauce
1 tsp chilli oil

1 tbsp tamarind paste
2 tbsp palm sugar or demerara sugar
2 cloves garlic, crushed

2 tbsp sunflower oil
225 g/8 oz baby onions
2 tbsp chopped fresh coriander
   (cilantro)

1 Using a sharp knife, thinly slice the beef.

2 Place the slices of beef in a large, shallow non-metallic dish.

3 Mix together the soy sauce, chilli oil, tamarind paste, palm sugar and garlic.

4 Spoon the palm sugar mixture over the beef. Toss well to coat the beef in the mixture, cover and leave to marinate for at least 1 hour.

5 Heat the sunflower oil in a preheated wok.

6 Peel the onions and cut them in half. Add the onions to the wok and stir-fry for 2–3 minutes, or until just browning.

7 Add the beef and marinade juices to the wok and stir-fry over a high heat for about 5 minutes.

8 Scatter with chopped fresh coriander (cilantro) and serve at once.

COOK'S TIP

Use the chilli oil carefully as it is very hot and could easily spoil the dish if too much is added.

Sweet Potato Stir-Fry with Coconut Beef

*This is a truly aromatic dish, blending the heat of red curry paste
with the aroma and flavour of the lime leaves and coconut.*

Serves 4

INGREDIENTS

2 tbsp vegetable oil
350 g/12 oz rump steak
2 cloves garlic
1 onion, sliced

350 g/12 oz sweet potato
2 tbsp Thai red curry paste
300 ml/½ pint/1¼ cups coconut
  milk

3 limes leaves
cooked jasmine rice, to serve

1 Heat the vegetable oil in a large preheated wok.

2 Using a sharp knife, thinly slice the beef. Add the beef to the wok and stir-fry for about 2 minutes or until sealed on all sides.

3 Add the garlic and the onion to the wok and stir-fry for a further 2 minutes.

4 Using a sharp knife, peel and dice the sweet potato.

5 Add the sweet potato to the wok with the curry paste, coconut milk and lime leaves and bring to a rapid boil. Reduce the heat, cover and leave to simmer for about 15 minutes or until the potatoes are tender.

6 Remove the lime leaves and transfer the stir-fry to warm serving bowls. Serve hot with cooked jasmine rice.

COOK'S TIP

There are two basic curry pastes used in Thai cuisine – red and green, depending on whether they are made from red or green chillies.

COOK'S TIP

If you cannot obtain lime leaves, use grated lime zest instead.

Beef with Green Peas & Black Bean Sauce

This recipe is the perfect example of quick stir-frying ingredients for a delicious, crisp, colourful dish.

Serves 4

INGREDIENTS

450 g/1 lb rump steak
2 tbsp sunflower oil
1 onion

2 cloves garlic, crushed
150 g/5$^{1}/_{2}$ oz/1 cup fresh or frozen
    peas

160 g/5$^{3}/_{4}$ oz jar black bean sauce
150 g/5$^{1}/_{2}$ oz Chinese leaves,
    shredded

1 Using a sharp knife, trim away any fat from the beef. Cut the beef into thin slices.

2 Heat the sunflower oil in a large preheated wok.

3 Add the beef to the wok and stir-fry for 2 minutes.

4 Using a sharp knife, peel and slice the onion.

5 Add the onion, garlic and peas to the wok and stir-fry for a further 5 minutes.

6 Add the black bean sauce and Chinese leaves to the mixture in the wok and heat through for a further 2 minutes or until the Chinese leaves have wilted.

7 Transfer to warm serving bowls and serve immediately.

COOK'S TIP

Chinese leaves are now widely available. They look like a pale, elongated head of lettuce with light green, tightly packed crinkly leaves.

COOK'S TIP

Buy a chunky black bean sauce if you can for the best texture and flavour.

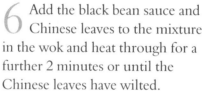

Stir-Fried Garlic Beef with Sesame Seeds & Soy Sauce

Soy sauce and sesame seeds are classic ingredients in Chinese cookery.
Use a dark soy sauce for fuller flavour and richness.

Serves 4

INGREDIENTS

25 g/1 oz/2 tbsp sesame seeds
450 g/1 lb beef fillet
2 tbsp vegetable oil

1 green (bell) pepper, deseeded and
thinly sliced
4 cloves garlic, crushed

2 tbsp dry sherry
4 tbsp soy sauce
6 spring onions (scallions), sliced
noodles, to serve

1 Heat a large wok until it is very hot.

2 Add the sesame seeds to the wok and dry fry, stirring, for 1–2 minutes or until they just begin to brown. Remove the sesame seeds from the wok and set aside until required.

3 Using a sharp knife, thinly slice the beef.

4 Heat the oil in the wok. Add the beef and stir-fry for 2–3 minutes or until sealed on all sides.

5 Add the sliced (bell) pepper and crushed garlic to the wok and continue stir-frying for 2 minutes.

6 Add the sherry and soy sauce to the wok together with the spring onions (scallions) and allow to bubble, stirring occasionally, for about 1 minute.

7 Transfer the garlic beef stir-fry to warm serving bowls and scatter with the dry-fried sesame seeds. Serve hot with boiled noodles.

COOK'S TIP

You can spread the sesame seeds out on a baking tray (cookie sheet) and toast them under a preheated grill (broiler) until browned all over, if you prefer.

Pork Fillet Stir-Fry with Crunchy Satay Sauce

Satay sauce is easy to make and is one of the best known and loved sauces in Oriental cooking. It is perfect with beef, chicken or pork as in this recipe.

Serves 4

INGREDIENTS

150 g/5^1/2 oz carrots
2 tbsp sunflower oil
350 g/12 oz pork neck fillet, thinly sliced
1 onion, sliced
2 cloves garlic, crushed

1 yellow (bell) pepper, deseeded and sliced
150 g/5^1/2 oz/2^1/3 cups mangetout (snow peas)
75 g/3 oz/1^1/2 cups fine asparagus chopped salted peanuts, to serve

SATAY SAUCE:
6 tbsp crunchy peanut butter
6 tbsp coconut milk
1 tsp chilli flakes
1 clove garlic, crushed
1 tsp tomato purée

1 Using a sharp knife, slice the carrots into thin sticks.

2 Heat the oil in a large wok. Add the pork, onion and garlic and stir-fry for 5 minutes or until the lamb is cooked through.

3 Add the carrots, (bell) pepper, mangetout (snow peas) and asparagus to the wok and stir-fry for 5 minutes.

4 To make the satay sauce, place the peanut butter, coconut milk, chilli flakes, garlic and tomato purée in a small pan and heat gently, stirring, until well combined.

5 Transfer the stir-fry to warm serving plates. Spoon the satay sauce over the stir-fry and scatter with chopped peanuts. Serve immediately.

COOK'S TIP

Cook the sauce just before serving as it tends to thicken very quickly and will not be spoonable if you cook it too far in advance.

Chinese Five Spice Crispy Pork with Egg Fried Rice

Pork is coated in a spicy mixture before being fried until crisp in this recipe and then stirred into a delicious egg rice for a very filling meal.

Serves 4

INGREDIENTS

275 g/9¹/₂ oz/1¹/₄ cups long-grain white rice
600 ml/1 pint/2¹/₂ cups cold water
350 g/12 oz pork tenderloin
2 tsp Chinese five spice powder
25 g/1 oz/4 tbsp cornflour (cornstarch)

3 large eggs, beaten
25 g/1 oz/2 tbsp demerara sugar
2 tbsp sunflower oil
1 onion
2 cloves garlic, crushed
100 g/3¹/₂ oz carrots, diced

1 red (bell) pepper, deseeded and diced
100 g/3¹/₂ oz/³/₄ cup peas
15 g/1 oz/2 tbsp butter
salt and pepper

1 Rinse the rice under cold running water. Place the rice in a large saucepan, add the cold water and a pinch of salt. Bring to the boil, cover, then reduce the heat and leave to simmer for about 9 minutes, or until all of the liquid has been absorbed and the rice is tender.

2 Meanwhile, slice the pork tenderloin into very thin pieces, using a sharp knife. Set aside until required.

3 Whisk together the five spice powder, cornflour (cornstarch), 1 egg and the demerara sugar. Toss the pork in the mixture until coated.

4 Heat the oil in a large wok. Add the pork and cook over a high heat until the pork is cooked through and crispy. Remove the pork from the wok with a slotted spoon and set aside.

5 Using a sharp knife, cut the onion into dice.

6 Add the onion, garlic, carrots, (bell) pepper and peas to the wok and stir-fry for 5 minutes.

7 Return the pork to the wok together with the cooked rice and stir-fry for 5 minutes.

8 Heat the butter in a frying pan (skillet). Add the remaining beaten eggs and cook until set. Turn out on to a clean board and slice thinly. Toss the strips of egg into the rice mixture and serve.

Spicy Pork Balls

*These small meatballs are packed with flavour and cooked
in a crunchy tomato sauce for a very quick dish.*

Serves 4

INGREDIENTS

450 g/1 lb pork mince
2 shallots, finely chopped
2 cloves garlic, crushed
1 tsp cumin seeds
1/2 tsp chilli powder

25 g/1 oz/1/2 cup wholemeal
  breadcrumbs
1 egg, beaten
2 tbsp sunflower oil
400 g/14 oz can chopped tomatoes,
  flavoured with chilli

2 tbsp soy sauce
200 g/7 oz can waterchestnuts,
  drained
3 tbsp chopped fresh coriander
  (cilantro)

1 Place the pork mince in a large mixing bowl. Add the shallots, garlic, cumin seeds, chilli powder, breadcrumbs and beaten egg and mix together well.

2 Take small pieces of the mixture and form into balls between the palms of your hands.

3 Heat the sunflower oil in a large preheated wok. Add the pork balls to the wok and stir-fry, in batches, over a high heat for about 5 minutes or until sealed on all sides.

4 Add the tomatoes, soy sauce and waterchestnuts and bring to the boil. Return the pork balls to the wok, reduce the heat and leave to simmer for 15 minutes.

5 Scatter with chopped fresh coriander (cilantro) and serve hot.

COOK'S TIP

Add a few teaspoons of chilli sauce to a tin of chopped tomatoes, if you can't find the flavoured variety.

COOK'S TIP

Coriander (cilantro) is also known as Chinese parsley, but has a much stronger flavour and should be used with care. Parsley is not a viable alternative, use basil if coriander (cilantro) is not available.

Sweet & Sour Pork

Everyone loves sweet and sour pork, a classic Chinese dish. Tender pork pieces are fried and served in a crunchy sauce. This dish is perfect served with plain rice.

Serves 4

INGREDIENTS

450 g/1 lb pork tenderloin
2 tbsp sunflower oil
225 g/8 oz courgettes (zucchini)
1 red onion, cut into thin wedges
2 cloves garlic, crushed
225 g/8 oz carrots, cut into thin sticks

1 red (bell) pepper, deseeded and sliced
100 g/3^{1}/$_{2}$ oz/1 cup baby corn corbs
100 g/3^{1}/$_{2}$ oz button mushrooms, halved
175 g/6 oz/1^{1}/$_{4}$ cups fresh pineapple, cubed

100 g/3^{1}/$_{2}$ oz/1 cup beansprouts
150 ml/^{1}/$_{4}$ pint/^{2}/$_{3}$ cup pineapple juice
1 tbsp cornflour (cornstarch)
2 tbsp soy sauce
3 tbsp tomato ketchup
1 tbsp white wine vinegar
1 tbsp clear honey

1 Using a sharp knife, thinly slice the pork tenderloin.

2 Heat the oil in a large preheated wok.

3 Add the pork to the wok and stir-fry for 10 minutes, or until the pork is completely cooked through and beginning to turn crispy at the edges.

4 Meanwhile, cut the courgettes (zucchini) into thin sticks.

5 Add the onion, garlic, carrots, courgettes (zucchini), (bell) pepper, corn cobs and mushrooms to the wok and stir-fry for a further 5 minutes.

6 Add the pineapple cubes and beansprouts to the wok and stir-fry for 2 minutes.

7 Mix together the pineapple juice, cornflour (cornstarch), soy sauce, ketchup, wine vinegar and honey.

8 Pour the sweet and sour mixture into the wok and cook over a high heat, tossing frequently, until the juices thicken. Transfer the sweet and sour pork to serving bowls and serve hot.

COOK'S TIP

If you prefer a crisper coating, toss the pork in a mixture of cornflour (cornstarch) and egg white and deep fry in the wok in step 3.

Twice-cooked Pork with (Bell) Peppers

This is a really simple yet colourful dish, the trio of (bell) peppers
off-setting the pork and sauce wonderfully.

Serves 4

INGREDIENTS

15 g/¹/₂ oz Chinese dried mushrooms
450g/1 lb pork leg steaks
2 tbsp vegetable oil
1 onion, sliced

1 red (bell) pepper, deseeded and
  diced
1 green (bell) pepper, deseeded and
  diced

1 yellow (bell) pepper, deseeded and
  diced
4 tbsp oyster sauce

1 Place the mushrooms in a large bowl. Pour over enough boiling water to cover and leave to stand for 20 minutes.

2 Using a sharp knife, trim any excess fat from the pork steaks. Cut the pork into thin strips.

3 Bring a large saucepan of water to the boil. Add the pork to the boiling water and cook for 5 minutes.

4 Remove the pork from the pan with a slotted spoon and leave to drain thoroughly.

5 Heat the oil in a large preheated wok. Add the pork to the wok and stir-fry for about 5 minutes.

6 Remove the mushrooms from the water and leave to drain thoroughly. Roughly chop the mushrooms.

7 Add the mushrooms, onion and the (bell) peppers to the wok and stir-fry for 5 minutes.

8 Stir in the oyster sauce and cook for 2-3 minutes. Transfer to serving bowls and serve immediately.

VARIATION

Use open-cap mushrooms, sliced, instead of Chinese mushrooms, if you prefer.

Pork with Mooli (White Radish)

Pork and mooli (white radish) are a perfect combination, especially with the added heat of the sweet chilli sauce.

Serves 4

INGREDIENTS

4 tbsp vegetable oil
450 g/1 lb pork tenderloin
1 aubergine (eggplant)

225 g/8 oz mooli (white radish)
2 cloves garlic, crushed

3 tbsp soy sauce
2 tbsp sweet chilli sauce

1 Heat 2 tablespoons of the vegetable oil in a large preheated wok

2 Using a sharp knife, thinly slice the pork.

3 Add the slices of pork to the wok and stir-fry for about 5 minutes.

4 Using a sharp knife, trim and dice the aubergine (eggplant). Peel and slice the mooli (white radish).

5 Add the remaining vegetable oil to the wok.

6 Add the diced aubergine (eggplant) to the wok together with the garlic and stir-fry for 5 minutes.

7 Add the mooli (white radish) to the wok and stir-fry for about 2 minutes.

8 Stir the soy sauce and sweet chilli sauce into the mixture in the wok and cook until heated through.

9 Transfer the pork and mooli (white radish) to warm serving bowls and serve immediately.

COOK'S TIP

Mouli (white radish) are long white vegetables common in Chinese cooking. They are generally available in most large supermarkets. They are usually grated and have a milder flavour than red radish.

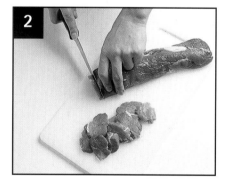

Lamb with Satay Sauce

This recipe demonstrates the classic serving of lamb satay, threaded on to wooden skewers having been marinated in a delicious chilli and coconut mixture.

Serves 4

INGREDIENTS

450 g/1 lb lamb loin fillet
1 tbsp mild curry paste
150 ml/5 fl oz/^{2}/$_3$ cup coconut milk
2 cloves garlic, crushed

^{1}/$_2$ tsp chilli powder
^{1}/$_2$ tsp cumin
1 tbsp corn oil
1 onion, diced

6 tbsp crunchy peanut butter
1 tsp tomato purée
1 tsp fresh lime juice
100 ml/3^1/$_2$ fl oz/1^1/$_3$ cup cold water

1 Using a sharp knife, thinly slice the lamb. Place the lamb in a large dish.

2 Mix together the curry paste, coconut milk, garlic, chilli powder and cumin in a bowl.

3 Pour the mixture over the lamb, toss well, cover and leave to marinate for 30 minutes.

4 Meanwhile, make the satay sauce. Heat the oil in a large wok. Add the onion and stir-fry for 5 minutes, then reduce the heat and cook for 5 minutes.

5 Add the peanut butter, tomato purée, lime juice and cold water to the wok, stirring well to combine.

6 Thread the lamb on to wooden skewers, reserving the marinade.

7 Grill (broil) the lamb skewers under a hot grill (broiler) for 6–8 minutes, turning once.

8 Add the reserved marinade to the wok, bring to the boil and cook for 5 minutes. Serve the lamb skewers with the satay sauce.

COOK'S TIP

Soak the wooden skewers in cold water for 30 minutes before grilling (broiling) to prevent the skewers from burning.

Stir-Fried Lamb with Black Bean Sauce & Mixed (Bell) Peppers

Red onions add great colour to recipes and are perfect in this dish, combining with the colours of the (bell) peppers.

Serves 4

INGREDIENTS

450 g/1 lb lamb neck fillet or
boneless leg of lamb chops
1 egg white, lightly beaten
25 g/1 oz/4 tbsp cornflour
(cornstarch)
1 tsp Chinese five spice powder

3 tbsp sunflower oil
1 red onion
1 red (bell) pepper, deseeded and
sliced
1 green (bell) pepper, deseeded and
sliced

1 yellow or orange (bell) pepper,
deseeded and sliced
5 tbsp black bean sauce
boiled rice or noodles, to serve

1 Using a sharp knife, slice the lamb into very thin strips.

2 Mix the egg white, cornflour (cornstarch) and Chinese five spice powder together in a large bowl. Toss the lamb strips in the mixture until evenly coated.

3 Heat the oil in a large preheated wok. Add the lamb and stir-fry over a high heat for 5 minutes or until it begins to crispen around the edges.

4 Using a sharp knife, slice the red onion. Add the onion and (bell) pepper slices to the wok and stir-fry for 5–6 minutes, or until the vegetables just begin to soften.

5 Stir the black bean sauce into the mixture in the wok and heat through.

6 Transfer the lamb and sauce to warm serving plates and serve hot with freshly boiled rice or noodles.

COOK'S TIP

Take care when frying the lamb as the cornflour (cornstarch) mixture may cause it to stick to the wok. Move the lamb around the wok constantly during stir-frying.

Spring Onion (Scallion) & Lamb Stir-Fry with Oyster Sauce

This really is a speedy dish, lamb leg steaks being perfect for the short cooking time.

Serves 4

INGREDIENTS

450 g/1 lb lamb leg steaks
1 tsp ground Szechuan peppercorns
1 tbsp groundnut oil

2 cloves garlic, crushed
8 spring onions (scallions), sliced
2 tbsp dark soy sauce

6 tbsp oyster sauce
175 g/6 oz Chinese leaves
prawn (shrimp) crackers, to serve

1 Using a sharp knife, remove any excess fat from the lamb. Slice the lamb thinly.

2 Sprinkle the ground Szechuan peppercorns over the meat and toss together until well combined.

3 Heat the oil in a preheated wok. Add the lamb and stir-fry for 5 minutes.

4 Mix the garlic, spring onions (scallions) and soy, add to the wok and stir-fry for 2 minutes.

5 Add the oyster sauce and Chinese leaves and stir-fry for a further 2 minutes, or until the leaves have wilted and the juices are bubbling.

6 Transfer the stir-fry to warm serving bowls and serve hot.

COOK'S TIP

Prawn (shrimp) crackers consist of compressed slivers of prawn (shrimp) and flour paste. They expand when deep-fried.

COOK'S TIP

Oyster sauce is made from oysters which are cooked in brine and soy sauce. Sold in bottles, it will keep in the refrigerator for months.

Curried Stir-Fried Lamb with Diced Potatoes

This dish is very filling, only requiring a simple vegetable accompaniment or bread.

Serves 4

INGREDIENTS

450 g/1 lb potatoes, diced
450 g/1 lb lean lamb, cubed
2 tbsp medium hot curry paste
3 tbsp sunflower oil

1 onion, sliced
1 aubergine (eggplant), diced
2 cloves garlic, crushed
1 tbsp grated fresh root ginger

150 ml/5 fl oz/²/3 cup lamb or beef stock
2 tbsp chopped fresh coriander (cilantro)

1 Bring a large saucepan of lightly salted water to the boil. Add the potatoes and cook for 10 minutes. Remove the potatoes from the saucepan with a slotted spoon and drain thoroughly.

2 Meanwhile, place the lamb in a large mixing bowl. Add the curry paste and mix until well combined.

3 Heat the sunflower oil in a large preheated wok.

4 Add the onion, aubergine (eggplant), garlic and ginger to the wok and stir-fry for about 5 minutes.

5 Add the lamb to the wok and stir-fry for a further 5 minutes.

6 Add the stock and cooked potatoes to the wok, bring to the boil and leave to simmer for 30 minutes, or until the lamb is tender and completely cooked through.

7 Transfer the stir-fry to warm serving dishes and scatter with chopped fresh coriander (cilantro). Serve immediately.

COOK'S TIP

The wok is an ancient Chinese invention, the name coming from the Cantonese, meaning a 'cooking vessel'.

Garlic-infused Lamb with Soy Sauce

The long marinating time allows the garlic to really penetrate the meat, creating a much more flavourful dish.

Serves 4

INGREDIENTS

450 g/1 lb lamb loin fillet
2 cloves garlic
2 tbsp groundnut oil
3 tbsp dry sherry or rice wine
3 tbsp dark soy
1 tsp cornflour (cornstarch)
2 tbsp cold water
25 g/1 oz/2 tbsp butter

1 Using a sharp knife, make small slits in the flesh of the lamb.

2 Carefully peel the cloves of garlic and cut them into slices, using a sharp knife.

3 Push the slices of garlic into the slits in the lamb. Place the garlic-infused lamb in a shallow dish.

4 Drizzle 1 tablespoon each of the oil, sherry and soy sauce over the lamb, cover and leave to marinate for at least 1 hour, preferably overnight.

5 Using a sharp knife, thinly slice the marinated lamb.

6 Heat the remaining oil in a preheated wok. Add the lamb and stir-fry for 5 minutes.

7 Add the marinade juices and the remaining sherry and soy sauce to the wok and allow the juices to bubble for 5 minutes.

8 Mix the cornflour (cornstarch) with the cold water. Add the cornflour (cornstarch) mixture to the wok and cook, stirring occasionally, until the juices start to thicken.

9 Cut the butter into small pieces. Add the butter to the wok and stir until the butter melts. Transfer to serving dishes and serve immediately.

COOK'S TIP

Adding the butter at the end of the recipe gives a glossy, rich sauce which is ideal with the lamb.

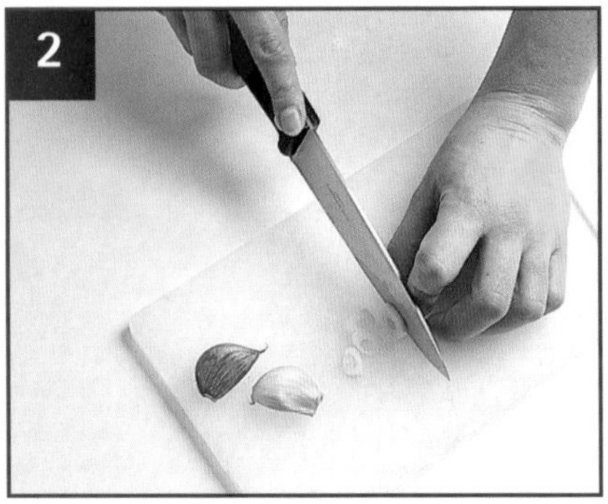

Thai-Style Lamb with Lime Leaves

*Groundnut oil is used here for flavour – it is
a common oil used for stir-frying.*

Serves 4

INGREDIENTS

2 red Thai chillies
2 tbsp groundnut oil
2 cloves garlic, crushed
4 shallots, chopped
2 stalks lemon grass, sliced

6 lime leaves
1 tbsp tamarind paste
25 g/1 oz/2 tbsp palm sugar
450 g/1 lb lean lamb (leg or loin fillet)

600 ml/1 pint/2$\frac{1}{2}$ cups coconut milk
175 g/6 oz cherry tomatoes, halved
1 tbsp chopped fresh coriander (cilantro)
fragrant rice, to serve

1 Using a sharp knife, deseed and very finely chop the Thai red chillies.

2 Heat the groundnut oil in a large preheated wok.

3 Add the garlic, shallots, lemon grass, lime leaves, tamarind paste, palm sugar and chillies to the wok and stir-fry for about 2 minutes.

4 Using a sharp knife, cut the lamb into thin strips or cubes.

5 Add the lamb to the wok and stir-fry for about 5 minutes, tossing well so that the lamb is evenly coated in the spice mixture.

6 Pour the coconut milk into the wok and bring to the boil. Reduce the heat and leave to simmer for 20 minutes.

7 Add the cherry tomatoes and chopped fresh coriander (cilantro) to the wok and leave to simmer for 5 minutes. Transfer to serving plates and serve hot with fragrant rice.

COOK'S TIP

Thai limes, also known as makut, *differ from the common lime in that the leaves are highly scented and the fruits resemble knobbly balls. Thai liime leaves are often used in cooking for flavour.*

Stir-Fried Lamb with Orange

Oranges and lamb are a great combination because the citrus flavour off-sets the fattier, fuller flavour of the lamb.

Serves 4

INGREDIENTS

450 g/1 lb minced lamb
2 cloves garlic, crushed
1 tsp cumin seeds
1 tsp ground coriander

1 red onion, sliced
finely grated zest and juice of
  1 orange
2 tbsp soy sauce

1 orange, peeled and segmented
salt and pepper
snipped fresh chives, to garnish

1 Add the minced lamb to a preheated wok. Dry fry the minced lamb for 5 minutes, or until the mince is evenly browned. Drain away any excess fat from the wok.

2 Add the garlic, cumin seeds, coriander and red onion to the wok and stir-fry for a further 5 minutes.

3 Stir in the finely grated orange zest and juice and the soy sauce, cover, reduce the heat and leave to simmer, stirring occasionally, for 15 minutes.

4 Remove the lid, raise the heat, add the orange segments and salt and pepper to taste and heat through for a further 2–3 minutes.

5 Transfer to warm serving plates and garnish with snipped fresh chives. Serve immediately.

COOK'S TIP

If you wish to serve wine with your meal, try light, dry white wines and lighter Burgundy-style red wines as they blend well with Oriental food.

VARIATION

Use lime or lemon juice and zest instead of the orange, if you prefer.

Lamb's Liver with Green (Bell) Peppers & Sherry

This is a richly flavoured dish which is great served with plain rice or noodles to soak up the delicious juices.

Serves 4

INGREDIENTS

450 g/1 lb lamb's liver
2 tbsp cornflour (cornstarch)
2 tbsp groundnut oil
1 onion, sliced

2 cloves garlic, crushed
2 green (bell) peppers, deseeded and sliced
2 tbsp tomato purée

3 tbsp dry sherry
1 tbsp cornflour (cornstarch)
2 tbsp soy sauce

1 Using a sharp knife, trim any excess fat from the lamb's liver. Slice the lamb's liver into thin strips.

2 Place the cornflour (cornstarch) in a large bowl.

3 Add the strips of lamb's liver to the cornflour (cornstarch) and toss well until coated evenly all over.

4 Heat the groundnut oil in a large preheated wok.

5 Add the lamb's liver, onion, garlic and green (bell) pepper to the wok and stir-fry for 6–7 minutes, or until the lamb's liver is just cooked through and the vegetables are tender.

6 Mix together the tomato purée, sherry, cornflour (cornstarch) and soy sauce. Stir the mixture into the wok and cook for a further 2 minutes or until the juices have thickened. Transfer to warm serving bowls and serve immediately.

VARIATION

Use rice wine instead of the sherry for a really authentic Oriental flavour. Chinese rice wine is made from glutinous rice and is also known as 'yellow wine' because of it's golden colour. The best variety, from south-east China, is called Shao Hsing *or* Shaoxing.

Fish & Seafood

Throughout the Far Eastern countries,
fish and seafood play a major role in the diet, as they
are both plentiful and healthy. There are many
different ways of cooking fish and seafood in a wok –
they may be steamed, deep-fried or stir-fried with a
range of delicious spices and sauces.

Japan is famed for its sushimi or raw fish, but this is
just one of the wide range of fish dishes served. Fish
and seafood are offered at every meal in Japan, many of
them cooked in a wok. Many unusual and tasty dishes
are offered in this chapter, combining fish and seafood
with aromatic herbs and spices, pastes and sauces.

When buying fish and seafood for the recipes in this
chapter, freshness is imperative to flavour, so be
sure to buy and use it as soon as possible,
preferably the same day.

Teriyaki Stir-Fried Salmon with Crispy Leeks

Teriyaki is a wonderful Japanese dish which is delicous when made with salmon and served on a bed of crispy leeks.

Serves 4

INGREDIENTS

450 g/1 lb salmon fillet, skinned
2 tbsp sweet soy sauce
2 tbsp tomato ketchup

1 tsp rice wine vinegar
1 tbsp demerara sugar
1 clove garlic, crushed

4 tbsp corn oil
450 g/1 lb leeks, thinly shredded
finely chopped red chillies, to garnish

1 Using a sharp knife, cut the salmon into slices. Place the slices of salmon in a shallow non-metallic dish.

2 Mix together the soy sauce, tomato ketchup, rice wine vinegar, sugar and garlic.

3 Pour the mixture over the salmon, toss well and leave to marinate for about 30 minutes.

4 Meanwhile, heat 3 tablespoons of the corn oil in a large preheated wok.

5 Add the leeks to the wok and stir-fry over a medium high heat for about 10 minutes, or until the leeks become crispy and tender.

6 Using a slotted spoon, carefully remove the leeks from the wok and transfer to warmed serving plates.

7 Add the remaining oil to the wok. Add the salmon and the marinade to the wok and cook for 2 minutes. Spoon over the leeks, garnish and serve immediately.

VARIATION

You can use a fillet of beef instead of the salmon, if you prefer.

Stir-Fried Salmon with Pineapple

Presentation plays a major part in Chinese cooking and this dish demonstrates this perfectly with the wonderful combination of colours.

Serves 4

INGREDIENTS

100 g/3³/₄ oz/1 cup baby corn cobs, halved

2 tbsp sunflower oil

1 red onion, sliced

1 orange (bell) pepper, deseeded and sliced

1 green (bell) pepper, deseeded and sliced

450 g/1 lb salmon fillet, skin removed

1 tbsp paprika

225 g/8 oz can cubed pineapple, drained

100 g/3¹/₂ oz/1 cup beansprouts

2 tbsp tomato ketchup

2 tbsp soy sauce

2 tbsp medium sherry

1 tsp cornflour (cornstarch)

1 Using a sharp knife, cut the baby corn cobs in half.

2 Heat the sunflower oil in a large preheated wok. Add the onion, (bell) peppers and baby corn cobs to the wok and stir-fry for 5 minutes.

3 Rinse the salmon fillet under cold running water and pat dry with absorbent kitchen paper.

4 Cut the salmon flesh into thin strips and place in a large bowl. Sprinkle with the paprika and toss until well coated.

5 Add the salmon to the wok together with the pineapple and stir-fry for a further 2–3 minutes or until the fish is tender.

6 Add the beansprouts to the wok and toss well.

7 Mix together the tomato ketchup, soy sauce, sherry and cornflour (cornstarch). Add the mixture to the wok and cook until the juices start to thicken. Transfer to warm serving plates and serve immediately.

VARIATION

You can use trout fillets instead of the salmon as an alternative, if you prefer.

Tuna & Vegetable Stir-Fry

*Fresh tuna is a dark, meaty fish and is now widely available at fresh fish counters.
It lends itself perfectly to the rich flavours in this recipe.*

Serves 4

INGREDIENTS

225 g/8 oz carrots
2 tbsp corn oil
1 onion, sliced
175 g/6 oz/2¹/₂ cups mangetout
  (snow peas)

175 g/6 oz/1³/₄ cups baby corn cobs,
  halved
450 g/1 lb fresh tuna
2 tbsp fish sauce
15 g/¹/₂ oz/1 tbsp palm sugar

finely grated zest and juice of
  1 orange
2 tbsp sherry
1 tsp cornflour (cornstarch)
rice or noodles, to serve

1 Using a sharp knife, cut the carrots into thin sticks.

2 Heat the corn oil in a large preheated wok.

3 Add the onion, carrots, mangetout (snow peas) and baby corn cobs to the wok and stir-fry for 5 minutes.

4 Using a sharp knife, thinly slice the tuna.

5 Add the tuna to the wok and stir-fry for 2–3 minutes, or until the tuna turns opaque.

6 Mix together the fish sauce, palm sugar, orange zest and juice, sherry and cornflour (cornstarch).

7 Pour the mixture over the tuna and vegetables and cook for 2 minutes, or until the juices thicken. Serve with rice or noodles.

COOK'S TIP

Palm sugar is a thick, coarse brown sugar that has a slightly caramel taste. It is sold in round cakes or in small, round, flat containers.

VARIATION

Try using swordfish steaks instead of the tuna. Swordfish steaks are now widely available and are similar in texture to tuna.

Stir-Fried Cod with Mango

Fish and fruit are a classic combination, and in this recipe a tropical flavour is added which gives a great scented taste to the dish.

Serves 4

INGREDIENTS

175 g/6 oz carrots
2 tbsp vegetable oil
1 red onion, sliced
1 red (bell) pepper, deseeded and
   sliced

1 green (bell) pepper, deseeded and
   sliced
450 g/1 lb skinless cod fillet
1 ripe mango
1 tsp cornflour (cornstarch)

1 tbsp soy sauce
100 ml/3^{1}/$_{2}$ fl oz/1^{1}/$_{3}$ cup tropical
   fruit juice
1 tbsp lime juice
1 tbsp chopped coriander (cilantro)

1 Using a sharp knife, slice the carrots into thin sticks.

2 Heat the vegetable oil in a preheated wok.

3 Add the onions, carrots and (bell) peppers to the wok and stir-fry for 5 minutes.

4 Using a sharp knife, cut the cod into small cubes.

5 Peel the mango, then carefully remove the flesh from the centre stone. Cut the flesh into thin slices.

6 Add the cod and mango to the wok and stir-fry for a further 4–5 minutes, or until the fish is cooked through. Do not stir the mixture too much or you may break the fish up.

7 Mix the cornflour (cornstarch), soy sauce, fruit juice and lime juice in a small bowl.

8 Pour the cornflour (cornstarch) mixture over the stir-fry and allow the mixture to bubble and the juices to thicken. Scatter with coriander (cilantro) and serve immediately.

VARIATION

You can use paw-paw (papaya) as an alternative to the mango, if you prefer.

Stir-Fried Gingered Monkfish

This dish is a real treat and is perfect for special occasions. Monkfish has a tender flavour which is ideal with asparagus, chilli and ginger.

Serves 4

INGREDIENTS

450 g/1 lb monkfish
1 tbsp freshly grated root ginger
2 tbsp sweet chilli sauce

1 tbsp corn oil
100 g/3¹/₂ oz/1 cup fine asparagus
3 spring onions (scallions), sliced

1 tsp sesame oil

1 Using a sharp knife, slice the monkfish into thin flat rounds.

2 Mix the ginger with the chilli sauce in a small bowl.

3 Brush the ginger and chilli sauce mixture over the monkfish pieces.

4 Heat the corn oil in a large preheated wok.

5 Add the monkfish, asparagus and spring onions (scallions) to the wok and stir-fry for about 5 minutes.

6 Remove the wok from the heat, drizzle the sesame oil over the stir-fry and toss well to combine.

7 Transfer to warm serving plates and serve immediately.

COOK'S TIP

Some recipes specify to grate ginger before it is cooked with other ingredients. To do this, just peel the flesh and rub it at a 45° angle up and down on the fine section of a metal grater, or use a special wooden or ceramic ginger grater.

VARIATION

Monkfish is quite expensive, but it is well worth using it as it has a wonderful flavour and texture. At a push you could use cubes of chunky cod fillet instead.

Braised Fish Fillets

Any white fish, such as lemon sole or plaice, is ideal for this delicious dish. Cornflour (cornstarch) paste is made by mixing 1 part cornflour (cornstarch) with about 1.5 parts cold water.

Serves 4

INGREDIENTS

3-4 small Chinese dried mushrooms
300-350 g/10$^{1}/_{2}$-12 oz fish fillets
1 tsp salt
$^{1}/_{2}$ egg white, lightly beaten
1 tsp cornflour (cornstarch) paste
600 ml/1 pint/2$^{1}/_{2}$ cups vegetable oil
1 tsp finely chopped ginger root

2 spring onions (scallions), finely chopped
1 garlic clove, finely chopped
$^{1}/_{2}$ small green (bell) pepper, deseeded and cut into small cubes
$^{1}/_{2}$ small carrot, thinly sliced
60 g/2 oz/$^{1}/_{2}$ cup canned sliced bamboo shoots, rinsed and drained

$^{1}/_{2}$ tsp sugar
1 tbsp light soy sauce
1 tsp rice wine or dry sherry
1 tbsp chilli bean sauce
2-3 tbsp Chinese stock or water
a few drops of sesame oil

1 Soak the dried mushrooms in a bowl of warm water for 30 minutes. Drain the mushrooms thoroughly on paper towels, reserving the soaking water for stock or soup. Squeeze the mushrooms to extract all of the moisture, cut off and discard any hard stems and slice thinly.

2 Cut the fish into bite-sized pieces, then place in a shallow dish and mix with a pinch of salt, the egg white and cornflour (cornstarch) paste, turning the fish to coat well.

3 Heat the oil in a preheated wok. Add the fish pieces to the wok and deep-fry for about 1 minute. Remove the fish pieces with a slotted spoon and leave to drain on paper towels.

4 Pour off the excess oil, leaving about 1 tablespoon in the wok. Add the ginger, spring onions (scallions) and garlic to flavour the oil for a few seconds, then add the (bell) pepper, carrots and bamboo shoots and stir-fry for about 1 minute.

5 Add the sugar, soy sauce, wine, chilli bean sauce, stock or water, and the remaining salt and bring to the boil. Add the fish pieces, stir to coat well with the sauce, and braise for 1 minute.

6 Sprinkle with sesame oil and serve immediately.

Fried Fish with Coconut & Basil

Fish curries are sensational and this Thai curry is no exception. Red curry and coconut are fantastic flavours with the fried fish.

Serves 4

INGREDIENTS

2 tbsp vegetable oil
450 g/1 lb skinless cod fillet
25 g/1 oz/$\frac{1}{4}$ cup seasoned flour
1 clove garlic, crushed

2 tbsp red Thai curry paste
1 tbsp fish sauce
300 ml/$\frac{1}{2}$ pint/$1\frac{1}{4}$ cups coconut
  milk

175 g/6 oz cherry tomatoes, halved
20 fresh basil leaves
fragrant rice, to serve

1   Heat the vegetable oil in a large preheated wok.

2   Using a sharp knife, cut the fish into large cubes, taking care to remove any bones with a pair of tweezers.

3   Place the seasoned flour in a bowl. Add the cubes of fish and mix until well coated.

4   Add the coated fish to the wok and stir-fry over a high heat for 3–4 minutes, or until the fish just begins to brown at the edges.

5   Mix together the garlic, curry paste, fish sauce and coconut milk in a bowl. Pour the mixture over the fish and bring to the boil.

6   Add the tomatoes to the mixture in the wok and leave to simmer for 5 minutes.

7   Roughly chop or tear the fresh basil leaves. Add the basil to the wok, stir carefully to combine, taking care not to break up the cubes of fish.

8   Transfer to serving plates and serve hot with fragrant rice.

COOK'S TIP

Take care not to overcook the dish once the tomatoes are added, otherwise they will break down and the skins will come away.

Coconut Prawns (Shrimp)

These crispy, fried prawns (shrimp) look fantastic and taste just as good. Fan-tail prawns (shrimp) make any meal a special occasion, especially when cooked in such a delicious crispy coating.

Serves 4

INGREDIENTS

50 g/1^3/$_4$ oz/^{1}/$_2$ cup desiccated (shredded) coconut
25 g/1 oz/^{1}/$_2$ cup fresh white breadcrumbs

1 tsp Chinese five spice powder
^{1}/$_2$ tsp salt
finely grated zest of 1 lime
1 egg white

450 g/1 lb fan-tail prawns (shrimp)
sunflower or corn oil, for frying
lemon wedges, to garnish

1 Mix together the dessicated (shredded) coconut, white breadcrumbs, Chinese five spice powder, salt and finely grated lime zest in a bowl.

2 Lightly whisk the egg white in a separate bowl.

3 Rinse the prawns (shrimp) under cold running water and pat dry with absorbent kitchen paper.

4 Dip the prawns (shrimp) into the egg white then into the coconut crumb mixture, so that they are evenly coated.

5 Heat about 5 cm/2 inches of sunflower or corn oil in a large preheated wok.

6 Add the prawns (shrimp) to the wok and stir-fry for about 5 minutes or until golden and crispy.

7 Remove the prawns (shrimp) with a slotted spoon, transfer to absorbent kitchen paper and leave to drain thoroughly.

8 Transfer the coconut prawns (shrimp) to warm serving dishes and garnish with lemon wedges. Serve immediately.

COOK'S TIP

Serve the prawns (shrimp) with a soy sauce or chilli sauce, if you wish.

Prawn (Shrimp) Omelette

*This really is a meal in minutes, combining many
Chinese ingredients for a truly tasty dish.*

Serves 4

INGREDIENTS

2 tbsp sunflower oil
4 spring onions (scallions), sliced
350 g/12 oz peeled prawns (shrimp)

100 g/3¹/₂ oz/1 cup beansprouts
1 tsp cornflour (cornstarch)
1 tbsp light soy sauce

6 eggs

1 Heat the sunflower oil in a large preheated wok.

2 Using a sharp knife, trim the spring onions (scallions) and cut into slices.

3 Add the prawns (shrimp), spring onions (scallions) and beansprouts to the wok and stir-fry for 2 minutes.

4 Mix together the cornflour (cornstarch) and soy sauce in a small bowl.

5 Beat the eggs with 3 tablespoons of cold water and

then blend with the cornflour (cornstarch) and soy mixture.

6 Add the egg mixture to the wok and cook for 5–6 minutes, or until the mixture sets.

7 Transfer the omelette to a serving plate and cut into quarters to serve.

COOK'S TIP

It is important to use fresh beansprouts for this dish as the canned ones don't have the crunchy texture necessary.

VARIATION

Add any other vegetables of your choice, such as grated carrot or cooked peas, to the omelette in step 3, if you wish.

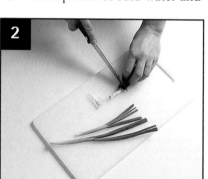

Prawns (Shrimp) with Spicy Tomatoes

*Basil and tomatoes are ideal flavourings for prawns (shrimp)
spiced with cumin seeds and garlic.*

Serves 4

INGREDIENTS

2 tbsp corn oil
1 onion
2 cloves garlic, crushed
1 tsp cumin seeds

1 tbsp demerara sugar
400 g/14 oz can chopped tomatoes
1 tbsp sundried tomato purée
1 tbsp chopped fresh basil

450 g/1 lb peeled king prawns
  (shrimp)
salt and pepper

1 Heat the corn oil in a large preheated wok.

2 Using a sharp knife, finely chop the onion.

3 Add the onion and garlic to the wok and stir-fry for 2–3 minutes, or until softened.

4 Stir in the cumin seeds and stir-fry for 1 minute.

5 Add the sugar, chopped tomatoes and sundried tomato purée to the wok. Bring the mixture to the boil, then reduce the heat and leave the sauce to simmer for 10 minutes.

6 Add the basil, prawns (shrimp) and salt and pepper to taste to the mixture in the wok. Increase the heat and cook for a further 2–3 minutes or until the prawns (shrimp) are completely cooked through.

COOK'S TIP

Always heat your wok before you add oil or other ingredients. This will prevent anything from sticking to it.

COOK'S TIP

Sundried tomato purée has a much more intense flavour than that of normal tomato purée. It adds a distinctive intensity to any tomato-based dish.

Prawns (Shrimp) with Crispy Ginger

Crispy ginger is a wonderful garnish which offsets the spicy prawns (shrimp) both visually and in flavour.

Serves 4

INGREDIENTS

5 cm/2 inch piece fresh root ginger
oil, for frying
1 onion, diced
225 g/8 oz carrots, diced

100 g/3^1/$_2$ oz/^{1}/$_2$ cup frozen peas
100 g/3^1/$_2$ oz/1 cup beansprouts
450 g/1 lb peeled king prawns
(shrimp)

1 tsp Chinese five spice powder
1 tbsp tomato purée
1 tbsp soy sauce

1 Using a sharp knife, peel the ginger and slice it into very thin sticks.

2 Heat about 2.5 cm/1 inch of oil in a large preheated wok.

3 Add the ginger to the wok and stir-fry for 1 minute or until the ginger is crispy. Remove the ginger with a slotted spoon and leave to drain on absorbent kitchen paper. Set aside.

4 Drain all of the oil from the wok except for about 2 tablespoons.

5 Add the onions and carrots to the wok and stir-fry for 5 minutes.

6 Add the peas and beansprouts to the wok and stir-fry for 2 minutes.

7 Rinse the prawns (shrimp) under cold running water and pat dry thoroughly with absorbent kitchen paper.

8 Mix together the five spice powder, tomato purée and soy sauce. Brush the mixture over the prawns (shrimp).

9 Add the prawns (shrimp) to the wok and stir-fry for a further 2 minutes, or until the prawns (shrimp) are completely cooked through. Transfer the prawn (shrimp) mixture to a warm serving bowl and top with the reserved crispy ginger. Serve immediately.

VARIATION

Use slices of white fish instead of the prawns (shrimp) as an alternative, if you wish.

Vegetables with Prawns (Shrimp) & Egg

*In this recipe, a light Chinese omelette is shredded and
tossed back into the dish before serving.*

Serves 4

INGREDIENTS

225 g/8 oz courgettes (zucchini)
3 tbsp vegetable oil
2 eggs
225 g/8 oz carrots, grated

1 onion, sliced
150 g/5^1/$_2$ oz/1^1/$_2$ cups beansprouts
225 g/8 oz peeled prawns (shrimp)
2 tbsp soy sauce

pinch of five spice Chinese powder
25 g/1 oz/^{1}/$_4$ cup peanuts, chopped
2 tbsp fresh chopped coriander
  (cilantro)

1 Finely grate the courgettes
(zucchini).

2 Heat 1 tablespoon of the oil
in a large preheated wok.

3 Beat the eggs with 2
tablespoons of cold water.
Pour the mixture into the wok and
cook for 2–3 minutes or until the
egg sets.

4 Remove the omelette from
the wok and transfer to a
clean board. Fold the omelette, cut
it into thin strips and set aside
until required.

5 Add the remaining oil to the
wok. Add the carrots, onion
and courgettes (zucchini) and stir-
fry for 5 minutes.

6 Add the beansprouts and
prawns (shrimp) to the wok
and cook for a further 2 minutes,
or until the prawns (shrimp) are
heated through.

7 Add the soy sauce, five spice
powder and peanuts to the
wok together with the strips of
omelette and heat through.
Garnish with chopped fresh
coriander (cilantro) and serve.

COOK'S TIP

*The water is mixed with the egg
in step 3 for a lighter, less
rubbery omelette.*

Stir-Fried Crab Claws with Chilli

Crab claws are frequently used in Chinese cooking, and look sensational.
They are perfect with this delicious chilli sauce.

Serves 4

INGREDIENTS

700 g/1 lb 9 oz crab claws
1 tbsp corn oil
2 cloves garlic, crushed
1 tbsp grated fresh root ginger

3 red chillies, deseeded and finely
  chopped
2 tbsp sweet chilli sauce
3 tbsp tomato ketchup

300 ml/$^1\!/_2$ pint/1$^1\!/_4$ cups cooled fish
  stock
1 tbsp cornflour (cornstarch)
salt and pepper
1 tbsp fresh chives, snipped

---

1 Gently crack the crab claws with a nut cracker. This process will allow the flavours of the chilli, garlic and ginger to fully penetrate the crab meat.

2 Heat the corn oil in a large preheated wok.

3 Add the crab claws to the wok and stir-fry for about 5 minutes.

4 Add the garlic, ginger and chillies to the wok and stir-fry for 1 minute, tossing the crab claws to coat all over.

5 Mix together the chilli sauce, tomato ketchup, fish stock and cornflour (cornstarch) in a small bowl.

6 Add the chilli and cornflour (cornstarch) mixture to the wok and cook, stirring occasionally, until the sauce starts to thicken. Season with salt and pepper to taste.

7 Transfer the crab claws and chilli sauce to warm serving dishes and garnish with plenty of snipped fresh chives. Serve immediately.

COOK'S TIP

If crab claws are not easily available, use a whole crab, cut into eight pieces, instead.

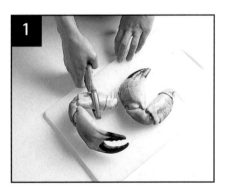

Chinese Leaves with Shiitake Mushrooms & Crab Meat

Chinese leaves and crab meat are a great combination as both have a delicate flavour which is enhanced by the coconut milk in this recipe.

Serves 4

INGREDIENTS

225 g/8 oz shiitake mushrooms
2 tbsp vegetable oil
2 cloves garlic, crushed
6 spring onions (scallions), sliced

1 head Chinese leaves, shredded
1 tbsp mild curry paste
6 tbsp coconut milk

200 g/7 oz can white crab meat, drained
1 tsp chilli flakes

1 Using a sharp knife, cut the the mushrooms into slices.

2 Heat the vegetable oil in a large preheated wok.

3 Add the mushrooms and garlic to the wok and stir-fry for 3 minutes or until the mushrooms have softened.

4 Add the spring onions (scallions) and shredded Chinese leaves to the wok and stir-fry until the leaves have wilted.

5 Mix together the mild curry paste and coconut milk in a small bowl.

6 Add the curry paste and coconut milk mixture to the wok together with the crab meat and chilli flakes. Mix together until well combined and heat through until the juices start to bubble.

7 Transfer to warm serving bowls and then serve immediately.

COOK'S TIP

Shiitake mushrooms are now readily available in the fresh vegetable section of most large supermarkets.

Stir-Fried Lettuce with Mussels & Lemon Grass

Mussels require careful preparation but very little cooking. They are available fresh or in vacuum packs when out of season.

Serves 4

INGREDIENTS

1 kg/2 lb 4oz mussels in their shells, scrubbed
2 stalks lemon grass, thinly sliced

2 tbsp lemon juice
100 ml/3^1/$_2$ fl oz/^{1}/$_3$ cup water
25 g/1 oz/2 tbsp butter

1 Iceberg lettuce
finely grated zest of 1 lemon
2 tbsp oyster sauce

1 Place the mussels in a large saucepan.

2 Add the lemon grass, lemon juice and water to the pan of mussels, cover with a tight-fitting lid and cook for 5 minutes or until the mussels have opened. Discard any mussels that do not open.

3 Carefully remove the cooked mussels from their shells, using a fork.

4 Heat the butter in a large preheated wok.

5 Add the lettuce and lemon zest to the wok and stir-fry for 2 minutes, or until the lettuce begins to wilt.

6 Add the oyster sauce to the mixture in the wok, stir and heat through. Serve immediately.

COOK'S TIP

Lemon grass with its citrus fragrance and lemon flavour looks like a fibrous spring onion (scallion) and is often used in Thai cooking.

COOK'S TIP

When using fresh mussels, be sure to discard any opened mussels before scrubbing and any unopened mussels after cooking.

Mussels in Black Bean Sauce with Spinach

This dish looks so impressive, the combination of colours making it look almost too good to eat!

Serves 4

INGREDIENTS

350 g/12 oz leeks
350 g/12 oz cooked green-lipped mussels (shelled)
1 tsp cumin seeds

2 tbsp vegetable oil
2 cloves garlic, crushed
1 red (bell) pepper, deseeded and sliced

50 g/1³/₄ oz/³/₄ cup canned bamboo shoots, drained
175 g/6 oz baby spinach
160 g/5³/₄ oz jar black bean sauce

1 Using a sharp knife, trim the leeks and shred them.

2 Place the mussels in a large bowl, sprinkle with the cumin seeds and toss well to coat all over.

3 Heat the vegetable oil in a large preheated wok.

4 Add the leeks, garlic and red (bell) pepper to the wok and stir-fry for 5 minutes, or until the vegetables are tender.

5 Add the bamboo shoots, baby spinach leaves and cooked green-lipped mussels to the wok and stir-fry for about 2 minutes.

6 Pour the black bean sauce over the ingredients in the wok, toss well to coat all over and leave to simmer for a few seconds, stirring occasionally.

7 Transfer the stir-fry to warm serving bowls and serve immediately.

COOK'S TIP

If the green-lipped mussels are not available they can be bought shelled in cans and jars from most large supermarkets.

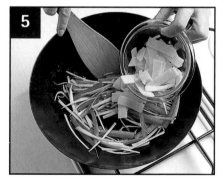

Scallop Pancakes

Scallops, like most shellfish require very little cooking, and this original and delicous dish is a perfect example of how to use shellfish to its full potential.

Serves 4

INGREDIENTS

100 g/3^1/$_2$ oz fine green beans
1 red chilli
450 g/1 lb scallops, without roe

1 egg
3 spring onions (scallions), sliced
50 g/1^3/$_4$ oz/^{1}/$_2$ cup rice flour

1 tbsp fish sauce
oil, for frying
sweet chilli dip, to serve

1 Using a sharp knife, trim the green beans and slice them very thinly.

2 Using a sharp knife, deseed and very finely chop the red chilli.

3 Bring a small saucepan of lightly salted water to the boil. Add the green beans to the pan and cook for 3–4 minutes or until just softened.

4 Roughly chop the scallops and place them in a large bowl. Add the cooked beans to the scallops.

5 Mix the egg with the spring onions (scallions), rice flour, fish sauce and chilli until well combined. Add to the scallops and mix well.

6 Heat about 2.5 cm/1 inch of oil in a large preheated wok. Add a ladleful of the mixture to the wok and cook for 5 minutes until golden and set. Remove the pancake from the wok and leave to drain on absorbent kitchen paper. Repeat with the remaining pancake mixture.

7 Serve the pancakes hot with a sweet chilli dip.

VARIATION

You could use prawns (shrimp) or shelled clams instead of the scallops, if you prefer.

Seared Scallops with Butter Sauce

Scallops have a terrific, subtle flavour which is complemented by this buttery sauce.

Serves 4

INGREDIENTS

450 g/1 lb scallops, without roe
6 spring onions (scallions)

2 tbsp vegetable oil
1 green chilli, deseeded and sliced

3 tbsp sweet soy sauce
50 g/1³/4 oz/1¹/2 tbsp butter, cubed

1 Rinse the scallops under cold running water, then pat the scallops dry with absorbent kitchen paper.

2 Using a sharp knife, slice each scallop in half horizontally.

3 Using a sharp knife, trim and slice the spring onions (scallions).

4 Heat the vegetable oil in a large preheated wok.

5 Add the chilli, spring onions (scallions) and scallops to the wok and stir-fry over a high heat for 4–5 minutes, or until the scallops are just cooked through.

6 Add the soy sauce and butter to the scallop stir-fry and heat through until the butter melts.

7 Transfer to warm serving bowls and serve hot.

COOK'S TIP

If you buy scallops on the shell, slide a knife underneath the membrane to loosen and cut off the tough muscle that holds the scallop to the shell. Discard the black stomach sac and intestinal vein.

COOK'S TIP

Use frozen scallops if preferred, but make sure they are completely defrosted before cooking. In addition, do not overcook them as they will easily disintegrate.

Stir-Fried Oysters with Tofu (Bean Curd), Lemon & Coriander (Cilantro)

Oysters are often eaten raw, but are delicious when quickly cooked as in this recipe, and mixed with salt and citrus flavours.

Serves 4

INGREDIENTS

225 g/8 oz leeks
350 g/12 oz tofu (bean curd)
2 tbsp sunflower oil
350 g/12 oz shelled oysters

2 tbsp fresh lemon juice
1 tsp cornflour (cornstarch)
2 tbsp light soy sauce
100 ml/3^1/$_2$ fl oz/^{1}/$_3$ cup fish stock

2 tbsp chopped fresh coriander
 (cilantro)
1 tsp finely grated lemon zest

1 Using a sharp knife, trim and slice the leeks.

2 Cut the tofu (bean curd) into bite-sized pieces.

3 Heat the sunflower oil in a large preheated wok.

4 Add the leeks to the wok and stir-fry for about 2 minutes.

5 Add the tofu (bean curd) and oysters to the wok and stir-fry for 1–2 minutes.

6 Mix together the lemon juice, cornflour (cornstarch), light soy sauce and fish stock in a small bowl.

7 Pour the cornflour (cornstarch) mixture into the wok and cook, stirring occasionally, until the juices start to thicken.

8 Transfer to serving bowls and scatter the coriander (cilantro) and lemon zest on top. Serve immediately.

VARIATION

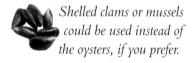

Shelled clams or mussels could be used instead of the oysters, if you prefer.

Crispy Fried Squid with Salt & Pepper

Squid tubes are classically used in Chinese cooking and are most attractive when presented as in the following recipe.

Serves 4

INGREDIENTS

450 g/1 lb squid, cleaned
25 g/1 oz/4 tbsp cornflour
(cornstarch)

1 tsp salt
1 tsp freshly ground black pepper
1 tsp chilli flakes

groundnut oil, for frying
dipping sauce, to serve

1 Using a sharp knife, remove the tentacles from the squid and trim. Slice the bodies down one side and open out to give a flat piece.

2 Score the flat pieces with a criss-cross pattern then cut each piece into 4.

3 Mix together the cornflour (cornstarch), salt, pepper and chilli flakes.

4 Place the salt and pepper mixture in a large polythene bag. Add the squid pieces and shake the bag thoroughly to coat the squid in the flour mixture.

5 Heat about 5 cm/2 inches of groundnut oil in a large preheated wok.

6 Add the squid pieces to the wok and stir-fry, in batches, for about 2 minutes, or until the squid pieces start to curl up. Do not overcook or the squid will become tough.

7 Remove the squid pieces with a slotted spoon, transfer to absorbent kitchen paper and leave to drain thoroughly.

8 Transfer to serving plates and serve immediately with a dipping sauce.

COOK'S TIP

Squid tubes may be purchased frozen if they are not available fresh. They are usually ready-cleaned and are easy to use. Ensure that they are completely defrosted before cooking.

Stir-Fried Squid with Green (Bell) Peppers & Black Bean Sauce

Squid really is wonderful if quickly cooked as in this recipe, and contrary to popular belief it is not tough and rubbery unless it is overcooked.

Serves 4

INGREDIENTS

450 g/1 lb squid rings
2 tbsp plain (all-purpose) flour
1/2 tsp salt

1 green (bell) pepper
2 tbsp groundnut oil
1 red onion, sliced

160 g/5 3/4 oz jar black bean sauce

1 Rinse the squid rings under cold running water and pat dry with absorbent kitchen paper.

2 Place the plain (all-purpose) flour and salt in a bowl and mix together. Add the squid rings and toss until they are finely coated.

3 Using a sharp knife, deseed the (bell) pepper. Slice the (bell) pepper into thin strips.

4 Heat the groundnut oil in a large preheated wok.

5 Add the (bell) pepper and red onion to the wok and stir-fry for about 2 minutes, or until the vegetables are just beginning to soften.

6 Add the squid rings to the wok and cook for a further 5 minutes, or until the squid is cooked through.

7 Add the black bean sauce to the wok and heat through until the juices are bubbling. Transfer to warm serving bowls and serve immediately.

COOK'S TIP

Serve this recipe with fried rice or noodles tossed in soy sauce, if you wish.

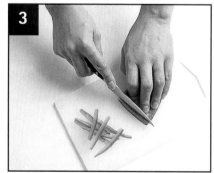

Vegetarian Dishes

As vegetables are so plentiful and diverse in the Far East, they play a major role in the diet. Other ingredients, such as tofu (bean curd), are added to the vegetarian diet, which is both a healthy and economical choice. Tofu (beancurd) is produced from the soya bean, which is grown in abundance in these countries. The cake variety of tofu (bean curd) is frequently used in stir-frying for texture and it is perfect for absorbing all of the component flavours of the dish.

The wok is perfect for cooking vegetables as it cooks them very quickly which helps to retain nutrients and crispness, and thus produces a range of colourful and flavourful recipes. Some of the dishes contained in this chapter are ideal accompaniments whilst others, such as vegetable curries, are combined with spices to produce more substantial main meals.

The following chapter shows the wonderful versatility of vegetables and contains something for everyone, which should delight vegetarians and meat-eaters alike.

Stir-Fried Japanese Mushroom Noodles

This quick dish is an ideal lunchtime meal, packed
with mixed mushrooms in a sweet sauce.

Serves 4

INGREDIENTS

250 g/9 oz Japanese egg noodles
2 tbsp sunflower oil
1 red onion, sliced
1 clove garlic, crushed

450 g/1 lb mixed mushrooms
(shiitake, oyster, brown cap)
350 g/12 oz pak choi (or Chinese
leaves)

2 tbsp sweet sherry
6 tbsp soy sauce
4 spring onions (scallions), sliced
1 tbsp toasted sesame seeds

1 Place the Japanese egg noodles in a large bowl. Pour over enough boiling water to cover and leave to soak for 10 minutes.

2 Heat the sunflower oil in a large preheated wok.

3 Add the red onion and garlic to the wok and stir-fry for 2–3 minutes, or until softened.

4 Add the mushrooms to the wok and stir-fry for about 5 minutes, or until the mushrooms have softened.

5 Drain the egg noodles thoroughly.

6 Add the the pak choi (or Chinese leaves), noodles, sweet sherry and soy sauce to the wok. Toss all of the ingredients together and stir-fry for 2–3 minutes or until the liquid is just bubbling.

7 Transfer the mushroom noodles to warm serving bowls and scatter with sliced spring onions (scallions) and toasted sesame seeds. Serve immediately.

COOK'S TIP

The variety of mushrooms in supermarkets has greatly improved and a good mixture should be easily obtainable. If not, use the more common button and flat mushrooms.

Stir-Fried Vegetables with Sherry & Soy Sauce

This is a simple, yet tasty side dish which is just as delicious as a snack or main course.

Serves 4

INGREDIENTS

2 tbsp sunflower oil
1 red onion, sliced
175 g/6 oz carrots, thinly sliced
175 g/6 oz courgettes (zucchini),
   sliced diagonally
1 red (bell) pepper, deseeded and
   sliced

1 small head Chinese leaves,
   shredded
150 g/5¹/₂ oz/3 cups beansprouts
225 g/8 oz can bamboo shoots,
   drained
150 g/5¹/₂ oz/¹/₄ cup cashew nuts,
   toasted

SAUCE:
3 tbsp medium sherry
3 tbsp light soy sauce
1 tsp ground ginger
1 clove garlic, crushed
1 tsp cornflour (cornstarch)
1 tbsp tomato purée

1 Heat the sunflower oil in a large preheated wok.

2 Add the red onion slices to the wok and stir-fry for 2–3 minutes, or until just beginning to soften.

3 Add the carrots, courgettes (zucchini) and (bell) pepper slices to the wok and stir-fry for a further 5 minutes.

4 Add the Chinese leaves, beansprouts and bamboo shoots to the wok and heat through for 2–3 minutes, or until the leaves just begin to wilt.

5 Scatter the cashew nuts over the top of the vegetables.

6 Mix together the sherry, soy sauce, ginger, garlic, cornflour (cornstarch) and tomato purée.

7 Pour the mixture over the vegetables and toss well. Leave to simmer for 2–3 minutes or until the juices start to thicken. Serve immediately.

COOK'S TIP

Use any mixture of fresh vegetables that you have to hand in this very versatile dish.

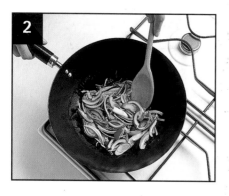

Stir-Fried Pak Choi with Red Onion & Cashew Nuts

Plum sauce is readily available in jars and has a terrific, sweet flavour which complements the vegetables.

Serves 4

INGREDIENTS

2 tbsp groundnut oil
2 red onions, cut into thin wedges

175 g/6 oz red cabbage, thinly shredded
225 g/8 oz pak choi

2 tbsp plum sauce
100 g/3½ oz/⅓ cup roasted cashew nuts

1 Heat the groundnut oil in a large preheated wok.

2 Add the onion wedges to the wok and stir-fry for about 5 minutes or until the onions are just beginning to brown.

3 Add the red cabbage to the wok and stir-fry for a further 2–3 minutes.

4 Add the pak choi to the wok and stir-fry for about 5 minutes, or until the leaves have wilted.

5 Drizzle the plum sauce over the vegetables, toss together until well combined and heat until the liquid is bubbling.

6 Scatter with the roasted cashew nuts and transfer to warm serving bowls. Serve immediately.

COOK'S TIP

Plum sauce has a unique, fruity flavour – a sweet and sour with a difference.

VARIATION

Use unsalted peanuts instead of the cashew nuts, if you prefer.

Tofu (Bean Curd) with Soy Sauce, Green (Bell) Peppers & Crispy Onions

Tofu (bean curd) is perfect for marinating as it readily absorbs flavours for a great tasting main dish.

Serves 4

INGREDIENTS

350 g/12 oz tofu (bean curd)
2 cloves garlic, crushed
4 tbsp soy sauce

1 tbsp sweet chilli sauce
6 tbsp sunflower oil
1 onion, sliced

1 green (bell) pepper, deseeded and diced
1 tbsp sesame oil

1 Using a sharp knife, cut the tofu (bean curd) into bite-sized pieces. Place the tofu (bean curd) pieces in a shallow non-metallic dish.

2 Mix together the garlic, soy sauce and sweet chilli sauce and drizzle over the tofu (bean curd). Toss well to coat each piece and leave to marinate for about 20 minutes.

3 Meanwhile, heat the sunflower oil in a large preheated wok.

4 Add the onion slices to the wok and stir-fry over a high heat until they brown and become crispy. Remove the onion slices with a slotted spoon and leave to drain on absorbent kitchen paper.

5 Add the tofu (bean curd) to the hot oil and stir-fry for about 5 minutes.

6 Remove all but 1 tablespoon of the oil from the wok. Add the (bell) pepper to the wok and stir-fry for 2–3 minutes, or until softened.

7 Return the tofu (bean curd) and onions to the wok and heat through, stirring occasionally. Drizzle with the sesame oil.

8 Transfer to serving plates and serve immediately.

COOK'S TIP

If you are in a real hurry, buy ready-marinated tofu (bean curd) from your supermarket.

Stir-Fried Green Beans with Lettuce & Blackbean Sauce

A terrific side dish, the variety of greens in this recipe make it as attractive as it is tasty.

Serves 4

INGREDIENTS

1 tsp chilli oil
25 g/1 oz/2 tbsp butter
225 g/8 oz fine green beans, sliced
4 shallots, sliced

1 clove garlic, crushed
100 g/3^1/2 oz shiitake mushrooms, thinly sliced
1 Iceberg lettuce, shredded

4 tbsp blackbean sauce

1 Heat the chilli oil and butter in a large preheated wok.

2 Add the green beans, shallots, garlic and mushrooms to the wok and stir-fry for 2–3 minutes.

3 Add the shredded lettuce to the wok and stir-fry until the leaves have wilted.

4 Stir the black bean sauce into the mixture in the wok and heat through, tossing to mix, until the sauce is bubbling. Serve.

COOK'S TIP

To make your own black bean sauce, soak 60 g/2 oz/^{1}/3 cup of dried black beans overnight in cold water. Drain and place in a pan of cold water, boil for 10 minutes, then drain. Return the beans to the pan with 450 ml/^{3}/4 pint/2 cups vegetable stock and boil. Blend 1 tbsp each of malt vinegar, soy sauce, sugar, 1^1/2 tsp cornflour (cornstarch), 1 chopped red chilli and ^{1}/2 inch ginger root. Add to the pan and simmer for 40 minutes.

COOK'S TIP

If possible, use Chinese green beans which are tender and can be eaten whole. They are available from specialist Chinese stores.

Deep-fried Courgettes (Zucchini)

These courgette (zucchini) fritters are irresistible and could be served
as a starter or snack with a chilli dip.

Serves 4

INGREDIENTS

450 g/1 lb courgettes (zucchini)
1 egg white

50 g/1³/4 oz/¹/3 cup cornflour
(cornstarch)
1 tsp salt

1 tsp Chinese five spice powder
oil, for deep-frying

1 Using a sharp knife, slice the courgettes (zucchini) into rings or chunky sticks.

2 Place the egg white in a small mixing bowl. Lightly whip the egg white until foamy, using a fork.

3 Mix the cornflour (cornstarch), salt and five spice powder and sprinkle on to a large plate.

4 Heat the oil for deep-frying in a large preheated wok.

5 Dip each piece of courgette (zucchini) into the beaten egg white then coat in the cornflour (cornstarch) mixture.

6 Deep-fry the courgettes (zucchini), in batches, for about 5 minutes or until pale golden and crispy. Repeat with the remaining courgettes (zucchini).

7 Remove the courgettes (zucchini) with a slotted spoon and leave to drain on absorbent kitchen paper while you deep-fry the remainder.

8 Transfer the courgettes (zucchini) to serving plates and serve immediately.

VARIATION

Alter the seasoning by using chilli powder or curry powder instead of the Chinese five spice powder, if you prefer.

Deep-fried Chilli Corn Balls

These small corn balls have a wonderful hot and sweet flavour, offset by the pungent coriander (cilantro) for a real taste of Thailand.

Serves 4

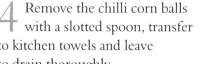

INGREDIENTS

6 spring onions (scallions), sliced
3 tbsp fresh coriander (cilantro), chopped
225 g/8 oz canned sweetcorn

5 ml/1 tsp mild chilli powder
1 tbsp sweet chilli sauce
25 g /1 oz/^{1}/$_4$ cup desiccated (shredded) coconut

1 egg
75 g/2^3/$_4$ oz/^{1}/$_3$ cup polenta (cornmeal)
oil, for deep-frying
extra sweet chilli sauce, to serve

1 In a large mixing bowl, mix together the spring onions (scallions), coriander (cilantro), sweetcorn, chilli powder, chilli sauce, coconut, egg and polenta (cornmeal). Cover and leave to stand for about 10 minutes.

2 Heat the oil for deep-frying in a large preheated wok.

3 Carefully drop spoonfuls of the chilli and polenta (cornmeal) mixture into the hot oil. Deep-fry the chill corn balls, in batches, for 4–5 minutes or until crispy and a deep golden brown colour.

4 Remove the chilli corn balls with a slotted spoon, transfer to kitchen towels and leave to drain thoroughly.

5 Transfer to serving plates and serve with an extra sweet chilli sauce for dipping.

COOK'S TIP

For safe deep-frying in a round-bottomed wok, place it on a wok rack so that it rests securely. Only half-fill the wok with oil. Never leave the wok unattended over a high heat.

COOK'S TIP

Polenta (cornmeal) is a type of meal ground from sweetcorn or maize. It is available in most large supermarkets or in health food shops.

Aspagarus & Red (Bell) Pepper Parcels

*These small parcels are ideal as part of a main meal and irresistible
as a quick snack with extra plum sauce for dipping.*

Serves 4

INGREDIENTS

100 g/3^1/$_2$ oz fine tip asparagus
1 red (bell) pepper, deseeded and
   thinly sliced

50 g/1^3/$_4$ oz/^{1}/$_2$ cup beansprouts
2 tbsp plum sauce
8 sheets filo pastry

1 egg yolk, beaten
oil, for deep-frying

1 Place the asparagus, (bell) pepper and beansprouts in a large mixing bowl.

2 Add the plum sauce to the vegetables and mix until well combined.

3 Lay the sheets of filo pastry out on to a clean work surface (counter).

4 Place a little of the asparagus and red (bell) pepper filling at the top end of each filo pastry sheet. Brush the edges of the filo pastry with a little of the beaten egg yolk.

5 Roll up the filo pastry, tucking in the ends and enclosing the filling like a spring roll.

6 Heat the oil for deep-frying in a large preheated wok.

7 Carefully cook the parcels, 2 at a time, in the hot oil for 4–5 minutes or until crispy.

8 Remove the parcels with a slotted spoon and leave to drain on absorbent kitchen paper.

9 Transfer the parcels to warm serving plates and serve immediately.

COOK'S TIP

Be sure to use fine-tipped asparagus as it is more tender than the larger stems.

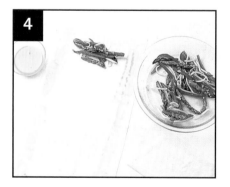

Carrot & Orange Stir-Fry

*Carrots and oranges have long been combined in Oriental cooking,
the orange juice bringing out the sweetness of the carrots.*

Serves 4

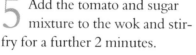
INGREDIENTS

2 tbsp sunflower oil	2 oranges, peeled and segmented	2 tbsp light soy
450 g/1 lb carrots, grated	2 tbsp tomato ketchup	100 g/3 1/2 oz/1/2 cup chopped
225 g/8 oz leeks, shredded	1 tbsp demerara sugar	peanuts

1 Heat the sunflower oil in a large preheated wok.

2 Add the grated carrot and leeks to the wok and stir-fry for 2–3 minutes, or until the vegetables have just softened.

3 Add the orange segments to the wok and heat through gently, ensuring that you do not break up the orange segments as you stir the mixture.

4 Mix the tomato ketchup, demerara sugar and soy sauce together in a small bowl.

5 Add the tomato and sugar mixture to the wok and stir-fry for a further 2 minutes.

6 Transfer the stir-fry to warm serving bowls and scatter with the chopped peanuts. Serve immediately.

VARIATION

You could use pineapple instead of orange, if you prefer. If using canned pineapple, make sure that it is in natural juice not syrup as it will spoil the fresh taste of this dish.

VARIATION

Scatter with toasted sesame seeds instead of the peanuts, if you prefer.

Spinach Stir-Fry with Shiitake & Honey

This stir-fry is the perfect accompaniment to tofu (bean curd) dishes, and it is so quick and simple to make.

Serves 4

INGREDIENTS

3 tbsp groundnut oil
350 g/12 oz shiitake mushrooms, sliced

2 cloves garlic, crushed
350 g/12 oz baby leaf spinach
2 tbsp dry sherry

2 tbsp clear honey
4 spring onions (scallions), sliced

1 Heat the groundnut oil in a large preheated wok.

2 Add the shiitake mushrooms to the wok and stir-fry for about 5 minutes, or until the mushrooms have softened.

3 Add the crushed garlic and baby leaf spinach to the mushrooms in the wok and stir-fry for a further 2–3 minutes, or until the spinach leaves have just wilted.

4 Mix together the dry sherry and clear honey in a small bowl until well combined.

5 Drizzle the sherry and honey mixture over the spinach and heat through.

6 Transfer the stir-fry to warm serving dishes and scatter with spring onions (scallion) slices. Serve immediately.

COOK'S TIP

Nutmeg complements the flavour of spinach and it is a classic combination. Add a pinch of nutmeg to the dish in step 3, if you wish.

COOK'S TIP

A good quality, dry pale sherry should be used in this recipe. Cream or sweet sherry should not be substituted. Rice wine is often used in Oriental cooking, but sherry can be used instead.

Chinese Vegetable Rice

This rice can either be served as a meal in itself or as an accompaniment to other vegetable recipes.

Serves 4

INGREDIENTS

350 g/12 oz/1³/₄ cups long-grain white rice

1 tsp turmeric

2 tbsp sunflower oil

225 g/8 oz courgettes (zucchini), sliced

1 red (bell) pepper, deseeded and sliced

1 green (bell) pepper, deseeded and sliced

1 green chilli, deseeded and finely chopped

1 medium carrot, coarsley grated

150 g/5¹/₂ oz/1¹/₂ cups beansprouts

6 spring onions (scallions), sliced, plus extra to garnish

2 tbsp soy sauce

1 Place the rice and turmeric in a saucepan of lightly salted water and bring to the boil. Reduce the heat and leave to simmer until the rice is just tender. Drain the rice thoroughly and press out any excess water with a sheet of double thickness kitchen paper.

2 Heat the sunflower oil in a large preheated wok.

3 Add the courgettes (zucchini) to the wok and stir-fry for about 2 minutes.

4 Add the (bell) peppers and chilli to the wok and stir-fry for 2–3 minutes.

5 Add the cooked rice to the mixture in the wok, a little at a time, tossing well after each addition.

6 Add the carrots, beansprouts and spring onions (scallions) to the wok and stir-fry for a further 2 minutes. Drizzle with soy sauce and serve at once, garnished with extra spring onions (scallions), if desired.

VARIATION

For real luxury, add a few saffron strands infused in boiling water instead of the turmeric.

Vegetable Stir-Fry with Hoisin Sauce

This vegetable stir-fry has rice aded to it and it can be served as a meal in itself.

Serves 4

INGREDIENTS

2 tbsp sunflower oil
1 red onion, sliced
100 g/3^1/$_2$ oz carrots, sliced

1 yellow (bell) pepper, deseeded and
  diced
50 g/1^3/$_4$ oz/1 cup cooked brown rice
175 g/6 oz mangetout (snow peas)

175 g/6 oz/1^1/$_2$ cups beansprouts
4 tbsp hoisin sauce
1 tbsp snipped fresh chives

1 Heat the sunflower oil in a large preheated wok.

2 Add the red onion slices, carrots and yellow (bell) pepper to the wok and stir-fry for about 3 minutes.

3 Add the cooked brown rice, mangetout (snow peas) and beansprouts to the mixture in the wok and stir-fry for a further 2 minutes.

4 Stir the hoisin sauce into the vegetables and mix until well combined and completely heated through.

5 Transfer to warm serving dishes and scatter with the snipped fresh chives. Serve immediately.

VARIATION

Almost any vegetables could be used in this dish: other good choices would be broccoli florets, baby corn cobs, green peas, Chinese leaves and young spinach leaves. Either white or black (oyster) mushrooms can also be used to give a greater diversity of textures. In addition, make sure that there is a good variety of colour in this dish.

COOK'S TIP

Hoisin sauce is a dark brown, reddish sauce made from soy beans, garlic, chilli and various other spices, and is commonly used in Chinese cookery. It may also be used as a dipping sauce.

Sweet & Sour Cauliflower & Coriander (Cilantro) Stir-Fry

Although sweet and sour flavourings are mainly associated with pork, they are ideal for flavouring vegetables as in this tasty recipe.

Serves 4

INGREDIENTS

450 g/1 lb cauliflower florets
2 tbsp sunflower oil
1 onion, sliced
225 g/8 oz carrots, sliced

100 g/3^1/$_2$ oz mangetout (snow peas)
1 ripe mango, sliced
100 g/3^1/$_2$ oz/1 cup beansprouts
3 tbsp chopped fresh coriander (cilantro)

3 tbsp fresh lime juice
1 tbsp clear honey
6 tbsp coconut milk

1 Bring a large saucepan of water to the boil. Add the cauliflower to the pan and cook for 2 minutes. Drain the cauliflower thoroughly.

2 Heat the sunflower oil in a large preheated wok.

3 Add the onion and carrots to the wok and stir-fry for about 5 minutes.

4 Add the drained cauliflower and mangetout (snow peas) to the wok and stir-fry for 2–3 minutes.

5 Add the mango and beansprouts to the wok and stir-fry for about 2 minutes.

6 Mix together the coriander (cilantro), lime juice, honey and coconut milk in a bowl.

7 Add the coriander (cilantro) mixture to the wok and stir-fry for about 2 minutes or until the juices are bubbling.

8 Transfer the stir-fry to serving dishes and serve immediately.

VARIATION

Use broccoli instead of the cauliflower as an alternative, if you prefer.

Broccoli & Chinese Leaves with Black Bean Sauce

Broccoli works well with the black bean sauce in this recipe, while the almonds add extra crunch and flavour.

Serves 4

INGREDIENTS

450 g/1 lb broccoli florets
2 tbsp sunflower oil
1 onion, sliced

2 cloves garlic, thinly sliced
25 g/1 oz/$^1/_4$ cup flaked (slivered) almonds

1 head Chinese leaves, shredded
4 tbsp black bean sauce

1 Bring a large saucepan of water to the boil. Add the broccoli florets to the pan and cook for 1 minute. Drain the broccoli thoroughly.

2 Meanwhile, heat the sunflower oil in a large preheated wok.

3 Add the onion and garlic to the wok and stir-fry until just beginning to brown.

4 Add the drained broccoli florets and the flaked almonds to the mixture in the wok and stir-fry for a further 2–3 minutes.

5 Add the Chinese leaves to the wok and stir-fry for a further 2 minutes.

6 Stir the black bean sauce into the vegetables in the wok, tossing to mix, and cook until the juices are just beginning to bubble.

7 Transfer the vegetables to warm serving bowls and serve immediately.

VARIATION

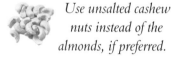

Use unsalted cashew nuts instead of the almonds, if preferred.

Chinese Mushrooms with Deep-fried Tofu (Bean Curd)

*Chinese mushrooms are available from Chinese supermarkets
and health food shops and add a unique flavour to Oriental dishes.*

Serves 4

INGREDIENTS

25 g/1 oz dried Chinese mushrooms
450 g/1 lb tofu (bean curd)
25 g/1 oz/4 tbsp cornflour
  (cornstarch)

oil, for deep-frying
2 cloves garlic, finely chopped
2.5 cm/1 inch piece of root ginger,
  grated

100 g/3^1/2 oz/^{3}/4 cup frozen or fresh
  peas

1 Place the Chinese mushrooms in a large bowl. Pour in enough boiling water to cover and leave to stand for about 10 minutes.

2 Meanwhile, cut the tofu (bean curd) into bite-sized cubes, using a sharp knife.

3 Place the cornflour (cornstarch) in a bowl.

4 Toss the tofu (bean curd) in the cornflour (cornstarch) until evenly coated.

5 Heat the oil for deep-frying in a large preheated wok.

6 Add the cubes of tofu (bean curd) to the wok and deep-fry, in batches, for 2–3 minutes or until golden and crispy. Remove the tofu (bean curd) with a slotted spoon and leave to drain on absorbent kitchen paper.

7 Drain off all but 2 tablespoons of oil from the wok. Add the garlic, ginger and Chinese mushrooms to the wok and stir-fry for 2–3 minutes.

8 Return the cooked tofu (bean curd) to the wok and add the peas. Heat through for 1 minute then serve hot.

COOK'S TIP

Use marinated tofu (bean curd) for extra flavour.

Stir-Fried Butternut Squash with Cashew Nuts & Coriander (Cilantro)

Butternut squash is as its name suggests, deliciously buttery and nutty in flavour. If the squash is not in season, use sweet potatoes instead.

Serves 4

INGREDIENTS

1 kg/2 lb 4oz butternut squash, peeled
3 tbsp groundnut oil
1 onion, sliced
2 cloves garlic, crushed
1 tsp coriander seeds

1 tsp cumin seeds
2 tbsp chopped coriander (cilantro)
150 ml/^{1}/$_4$ pint/^{2}/$_3$ cup coconut milk
100 ml/3^1/$_2$ fl oz/^{1}/$_2$ cup water
100 g/3^1/$_2$ oz/^{1}/$_3$ cup salted cashew nuts

TO GARNISH:
freshly grated lime zest
fresh coriander (cilantro)
lime wedges

1 Using a sharp knife, slice the butternut squash into small, bite-sized cubes.

2 Heat the groundnut oil in a large preheated wok.

3 Add the squash, onion and garlic to the wok and stir-fry for 5 minutes.

4 Stir in the coriander seeds, cumin and fresh coriander (cilantro) and stir-fry for 1 minute.

5 Add the coconut milk and water to the wok and bring to the boil. Cover the wok and leave to simmer for 10–15 minutes, or until the squash is tender.

6 Add the cashew nuts and stir to combine.

7 Transfer to warm serving dishes and garnish with freshly grated lime zest, fresh coriander (cilantro) and lime wedges. Serve hot.

COOK'S TIP

If you do not have coconut milk, grate some creamed coconut into the dish with the water in step 5.

Quorn with Ginger & Mixed Vegetables

Quorn, like tofu (bean curd), absorbs all of the flavours in a dish, making it ideal for this recipe which is packed with classic Chinese flavourings.

Serves 4

INGREDIENTS

1 tbsp grated fresh root ginger
1 tsp ground ginger
1 tbsp tomato purée
2 tbsp sunflower oil

1 clove garlic, crushed
2 tbsp soy sauce
350 g/12 oz Quorn or soya cubes
225 g/8 oz carrots, sliced

100 g/3^1/$_2$ oz green beans, sliced
4 stalks celery, sliced
1 red (bell) pepper, deseeded and sliced
boiled rice, to serve

1 Place the grated fresh ginger, ground ginger, tomato purée, 1 tablespoon of the sunflower oil, garlic, soy sauce and Quorn or soya cubes in a large bowl. Mix well to combine, stirring carefully so that you don't break up the Quorn or soya cubes. Cover and leave to marinate for 20 minutes.

2 Heat the remaining sunflower oil in a large preheated wok.

3 Add the marinated Quorn mixture to the wok and stir-fry for about 2 minutes.

4 Add the carrots, green beans, celery and red (bell) pepper to the wok and stir-fry for a further 5 minutes.

5 Transfer the stir-fry to warm serving dishes and serve immediately with freshly cooked boiled rice.

COOK'S TIP

Ginger root will keep for several weeks in a cool, dry place. Ginger root can also be kept frozen – break off lumps as needed.

VARIATION

Use tofu (bean curd) instead of the Quorn, if you prefer.

Leeks with Baby Corn Cobs & Yellow Bean Sauce

This is a simple side dish which is ideal with other main meal vegetarian dishes.

Serves 4

INGREDIENTS

3 tbsp groundnut oil
450 g/1 lb leeks, sliced

225 g/8 oz Chinese leaves, shredded
175 g/6 oz baby corn cobs, halved

6 spring onions (scallions), sliced
4 tbsp yellow bean sauce

1 Heat the groundnut oil in a large preheated wok.

2 Add the leeks, shredded Chinese leaves and baby corn cobs to the wok and stir-fry over a high heat for about 5 minutes or until the edges of the vegetables are slightly brown.

3 Add the spring onions (scallions) to the wok, stirring to combine.

4 Add the yellow bean sauce to the mixture in the wok and stir-fry for a further 2 minutes, or until heated through.

5 Transfer to warm serving dishes and serve immediately.

COOK'S TIP

Yellow bean sauce adds an authentic Chinese flavour to stir-fries. It is made from crushed salted soya beans mixed with flour and spices to make a thick paste. It is mild in flavour and is excellent with a range of vegetables.

COOK'S TIP

Baby corn cobs are sweeter and have a more delicate flavour than the larger corn cobs and are therefore perfect for stir-frying.

Vegetable Stir-Fry

A range of delicious flavours are captured in this simple recipe which is ideal if you are in a hurry.

Serves 4

INGREDIENTS

3 tbsp olive oil
8 baby onions, halved
1 aubergine (eggplant), cubed
225 g/8 oz courgettes (zucchini), sliced

225 g/8 oz open-cap mushrooms, halved
2 cloves garlic, crushed
400 g/14 oz can chopped tomatoes
2 tbsp sundried tomato purée

freshly ground black pepper
fresh basil leaves, to garnish

1 Heat the olive oil in a large preheated wok.

2 Add the baby onions and aubergine (eggplant) to the wok and stir-fry for 5 minutes, or until the vegetables are golden and just beginning to soften.

3 Add the courgettes (zucchini), mushrooms, garlic, tomatoes and tomato purée to the wok and stir-fry for about 5 minutes. Reduce the heat and leave to simmer for 10 minutes, or until the vegetables are tender.

4 Season with freshly ground black pepper and scatter with fresh basil leaves. Serve immediately.

COOK'S TIP

Wok cooking is an excellent means of cooking for vegetarians as it is a quick and easy way of serving up delicious dishes of crisp, tasty vegetables. All ingredients should be cut into uniform sizes with as many cut surfaces exposed as possible for quick cooking.

VARIATION

If you want to serve this as a vegetarian main meal, add cubed tofu (bean curd) in step 3.

Stir-Fried (Bell) Pepper Trio with Chestnuts & Garlic

*This a crisp and colourful recipe, topped with crisp,
shredded leeks for both flavour and colour.*

Serves 4

INGREDIENTS

225 g/8 oz leeks
oil, for deep-frying
3 tbsp groundnut oil
1 yellow (bell) pepper, deseeded and
   diced

1 green (bell) pepper, deseeded and
   diced
1 red (bell) pepper, deseeded and
   diced

200 g/7 oz can waterchestnuts,
   drained and sliced
2 cloves garlic, crushed
3 tbsp light soy sauce

1 To make the garnish, finely
slice the leeks into thin strips,
using a sharp knife.

2 Heat the oil for deep-frying
in a wok and cook the leeks
for 2–3 minute, or until crispy.
Set the crispy leeks aside until
required.

3 Heat the 3 tablespoons of
groundnut oil in the wok.

4 Add the (bell) peppers to the
wok and stir-fry over a high
heat for about 5 minutes, or until
they are just beginning to brown at
the edges and to soften.

5 Add the sliced waterchestnuts,
garlic and light soy sauce
to the wok and stir-fry all of
the vegetables for a further
2–3 minutes.

6 Spoon the (bell) pepper stir-
fry on to warm serving plates.

7 Garnish the stir-fry with the
crispy leeks.

VARIATION

*Add 1 tbsp of hoisin sauce with
the soy sauce in step 5 for extra
flavour and spice.*

Spiced Aubergine (Eggplant) Stir-Fry

This is a spicy and sweet dish, flavoured with mango chutney and heated up with chillies for a really wonderful combination of flavours.

Serves 4

INGREDIENTS

3 tbsp groundnut oil
2 onions, sliced
2 cloves garlic, chopped
2 aubergines (eggplants), diced

2 red chillies, deseeded and very
  finely chopped
2 tbsp demerara sugar
6 spring onions (scallions), sliced

3 tbsp mango chutney
oil, for deep-frying
2 cloves garlic, sliced, to garnish

1 Heat the groundnut oil in a large preheated wok.

2 Add the onions and chopped garlic to the wok, stirring well.

3 Add the aubergine (eggplant) and chillies to the wok and stir-fry for 5 minutes.

4 Add the sugar, spring onions (scallions) and mango chutney to the wok, stirring well. Reduce the heat, cover and leave to simmer, stirring from time to time, for 15 minutes or until the aubergine (eggplant) is tender.

5 Transfer the stir-fry to serving bowls and keep warm. Heat the oil for deep-frying in the wok and quickly stir-fry the slices of garlic. Garnish the stir-fry with the deep-fried garlic and serve immediately.

COOK'S TIP

The 'hotness' of chillies varies enormously so always use with caution, but as a general guide the smaller they are the hotter they will be. The seeds are the hottest part and so are usually discarded.

COOK'S TIP

Keep the vegetables moving around the wok as the aubergines (eggplant) will soak up the oil very quickly and may begin to burn if left unattended.

Stir-Fried Vegetables with Peanuts & Eggs

Known as Gado Gado in China, this is a true classic which never fades from popularity.
A delicious warm salad with a peanut sauce.

Serves 4

INGREDIENTS

2 eggs	2 tbsp vegetable oil	1 tbsp tomato ketchup
225 g/8 oz carrots	1 red (bell) pepper, deseeded and	2 tbsp soy sauce
350 g/12 oz white cabbage	thinly sliced	75 g/2^3/$_4$ oz/^{1}/$_3$ cup salted peanuts,
	150 g/5^1/$_2$ oz/1^1/$_2$ cups beansprouts	chopped

1 Bring a small saucepan of water to the boil. Add the eggs to the pan and cook for about 7 minutes. Remove the eggs from the pan and leave to cool under cold running water for 1 minute.

2 Peel the shell from the eggs and then cut the eggs into quarters.

3 Peel and coarsley grate the carrots.

4 Using a sharp knife, thinly shred the white cabbage.

5 Heat the vegetable oil in a large preheated wok.

6 Add the carrots, white cabbage and (bell) pepper to the wok and stir-fry for 3 minutes.

7 Add the beansprouts to the wok and stir-fry for 2 minutes.

8 Add the tomato ketchup, soy sauce and peanuts to the wok and stir-fry for 1 minute.

9 Transfer the stir-fry to warm serving plates and garnish with the hard-boiled (hard-cooked) egg quarters. Serve immediately.

COOK'S TIP

The eggs are cooled in cold water immediately after cooking in order to prevent the egg yolk blackening around the edges.

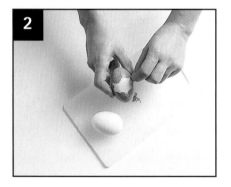

Rice & Noodles

Rice and noodles are staples in the Far East, as they are cheap, plentiful, nutritious and delicious. They are such versatile ingredients and are therefore always served as part of a meal. Many rice and noodle dishes are served as accompaniments and others as main dishes with meat, vegetables and fish flavoured with spices and seasonings.

There are several types of rice grown and used in the various Far Eastern countries, each perfect for its specific use. Due to the climates of these countries and the perfect rice-growing conditions, natives have adapted recipes to suit their own individual tastes. Plain rice is served to punctuate a meal and settle the stomach during larger meals.

Noodles vary from country to country and are eaten day and night in various forms. Thin egg noodles are made from wheat flour, water and egg and are probably the most common in the Western diet. They are available both fresh and dried and require very little cooking. Rice noodles are also widely used, known as sha he *in China and* harusame *in Japan. Mung beans are also ground to produce cellophane or transparent noodles which are perfect for reheating and adding to recipes.*

Fried Rice with Spicy Beans

This rice is really colourful and crunchy with the addition of sweetcorn and red kidney beans.
It may be served as a main vegetarian dish or as a side dish with meat or fish.

Serves 4

INGREDIENTS

3 tbsp sunflower oil
1 onion, finely chopped
225 g/8 oz/1 cup long-grain white
   rice

1 green (bell) pepper, deseeded and
   diced
1 tsp chilli powder
600 ml/1 pint/2^1/$_2$ cups boiling water

100 g/3^1/$_2$ oz canned sweetcorn
225 g/8 oz canned red kidney beans
2 tbsp chopped fresh coriander
   (cilantro)

1 Heat the sunflower oil in a large preheated wok.

2 Add the finely chopped onion to the wok and stir-fry for about 2 minutes or until the onion has softened.

3 Add the long-grain rice, diced (bell) pepper and chilli powder to the wok and stir-fry for 1 minute.

4 Pour 600 ml/1 pint/2^1/$_2$ cups of boiling water into the wok. Bring to the boil, then reduce the heat and leave the mixture to simmer for 15 minutes.

5 Add the sweetcorn, kidney beans and coriander (cilantro) to the wok and heat through, stirring occasionally.

6 Transfer to a serving bowl and serve hot, scattered with extra coriander (cilantro), if wished.

COOK'S TIP

For perfect fried rice, the raw rice should ideally be soaked in a bowl of water for a short time before cooking to remove excess starch. Short-grain Oriental rice can be substituted for the long-grain rice.

VARIATION

For extra heat, add 1 chopped red chilli as well as the chilli powder in step 3.

Coconut Rice

This fragrant, sweet rice is delicious served with meat, vegetable or fish dishes as part of a Thai menu.

Serves 4

INGREDIENTS

275 g/9^1/$_2$ oz long-grain white rice
600 ml/1 pint/2^1/$_2$ cups water

^{1}/$_2$ tsp salt
100 ml/3^1/$_2$ fl oz/^{1}/$_3$ cup coconut milk

25 g/1 oz/^{1}/$_4$ cup desiccated (shredded) coconut

1 Rinse the rice thoroughly under cold running water until the water runs clear.

2 Drain the rice thoroughly in a sieve set over a large bowl.

3 Place the rice in a wok with 600 ml/1 pint/2^1/$_2$ cups water.

4 Add the salt and coconut milk to the wok and bring to the boil. Cover the wok, reduce the heat and leave to simmer for 10 minutes.

5 Remove the lid from the wok and fluff up the rice with a fork – all of the liquid should be absorbed and the rice grains should be tender.

6 Spoon the coconut rice into a warm serving bowl and scatter with the desiccated (shredded) coconut. Serve immediately.

COOK'S TIP

Coconut milk is not the liquid found inside coconuts – that is called coconut water. Coconut milk is made from the white coconut flesh soaked in water and milk and then squeezed to extract all of the flavour. You can make your own or buy it in cans.

COOK'S TIP

The rice is rinsed under cold running water to remove some of the starch and to prevent the grains from sticking together.

Stir-Fried Onion Rice with Five Spice Chicken

This dish has a wonderful colour obtained from the turmeric, and a great spicy flavour, making it very appealing all round.

Serves 4

INGREDIENTS

1 tbsp Chinese five spice powder
2 tbsp cornflour (cornstarch)
350 g/12 oz boneless, skinless
    chicken breasts, cubed

3 tbsp groundnut oil
1 onion, diced
225 g/8 oz/1 cup long-grain white
    rice

$^1/_2$ tsp tumeric
600 ml/1 pint/$2^1/_2$ cups chicken stock
2 tbsp snipped fresh chives

1 Place the Chinese five spice powder and cornflour (cornstarch) in a large bowl. Add the chicken pieces and toss to coat all over.

2 Heat 2 tablespoons of the groundnut oil in a large preheated wok. Add the chicken pieces to the wok and stir-fry for 5 minutes. Using a slotted spoon, remove the chicken and set aside.

3 Add the remaining groundnut oil to the wok.

4 Add the onion to the wok and stir-fry for 1 minute.

5 Add the rice, tumeric and chicken stock to the wok and bring to the boil.

6 Return the chicken pieces to the wok, reduce the heat and leave to simmer for 10 minutes, or until the liquid has been absorbed and the rice is tender.

7 Add the chives, stir to mix and serve hot.

COOK'S TIP

Be careful when using turmeric as it can stain the hands and clothes a distinctive shade of yellow.

Chinese Chicken Rice

*This is a really colourful main meal or side dish
which tastes just as good as it looks.*

Serves 4

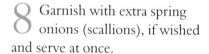
INGREDIENTS

350 g/12 oz/1³/₄ cups long-grain
  white rice
1 tsp turmeric
2 tbsp sunflower oil
350 g/12 oz skinless, boneless
  chicken breasts or thighs, sliced

1 red (bell) pepper, deseeded and
  sliced
1 green (bell) pepper, deseeded and
  sliced
1 green chilli, deseeded and finely
  chopped

1 medium carrot, coarsely grated
150 g/5¹/₂ oz/1¹/₂ cups beansprouts
6 spring onions (scallions), sliced,
  plus extra to garnish
2 tbsp soy sauce

1 Place the rice and turmeric in a large saucepan of lightly salted water and cook until the grains of rice are just tender, about 10 minutes. Drain the rice thoroughly and press out any excess water with double thickness paper towels.

2 Heat the sunflower oil in a large preheated wok.

3 Add the strips of chicken to the wok and stir-fry over a high heat until the chicken is just beginning to turn a golden colour.

4 Add the (bell) peppers and chilli to the wok and stir-fry for 2–3 minutes.

5 Add the rice to the wok, a little at a time, tossing well after each addition until well combined.

6 Add the carrot, beansprouts and spring onions (scallions) to the wok and stir-fry for a further 2 minutes.

7 Drizzle with the soy sauce and mix well.

8 Garnish with extra spring onions (scallions), if wished and serve at once.

VARIATION

Use pork marinated in hoisin sauce instead of the chicken, if you prefer.

Sweet Chilli Pork Fried Rice

*This is a variation of egg fried rice which may be served
as an accompaniment to a main meal dish.*

Serves 4

INGREDIENTS

450 g/1 lb pork tenderloin
2 tbsp sunflower oil
2 tbsp sweet chilli sauce, plus extra
   to serve
1 onion, sliced

175 g/6 oz carrots, cut into thin
   sticks
175 g/6 oz courgettes (zucchini), cut
   into sticks
100 g/3$^{1}/_{2}$ oz/1 cup canned bamboo
   shoots, drained

275 g/9$^{1}/_{2}$ oz/4$^{3}/_{4}$ cups cooked long-
   grain rice
1 egg, beaten
1 tbsp chopped fresh parsley

1 Using a sharp knife, slice the pork thinly.

2 Heat the sunflower oil in a large preheated wok.

3 Add the pork to the wok and stir-fry for 5 minutes.

4 Add the chilli sauce to the wok and allow to bubble, stirring, for 2–3 minutes or until syrupy.

5 Add the onions, carrots, courgettes (zucchini) and

bamboo shoots to the wok and stir-fry for a further 3 minutes.

6 Add the cooked rice and stir-fry for 2–3 minutes, or until the rice is heated through.

7 Drizzle the beaten egg over the top of the fried rice and cook, tossing the ingredients in the wok, until the egg sets.

8 Scatter with chopped fresh parsley and serve immediately, with extra sweet chilli sauce, if desired.

COOK'S TIP

*For a really quick dish, add frozen
mixed vegetables to the rice instead
of the freshly prepared vegetables.*

Egg Fried Rice with Seven Spice Beef

*Beef fillet is used in this recipe as it is very suitable
for quick cooking and has a wonderful flavour.*

Serves 4

INGREDIENTS

225 g/8 oz/1 cup long-grain white
  rice
600 ml/1 pint/2^1/$_2$ cups water
350 g/12 oz beef fillet
2 tbsp soy sauce

2 tbsp tomato ketchup
1 tbsp Thai seven spice seasoning
2 tbsp groundnut oil
1 onion, diced

225 g/8 oz carrots, diced
100 g/3^1/$_2$ oz/^{3}/$_4$ cup frozen peas
2 eggs, beaten
2 tbsp cold water

1 Rinse the rice under cold running water, then drain thoroughly. Place the rice in a saucepan with 600 ml/1 pint/2^1/$_2$ cups of water, bring to the boil, cover and leave to simmer for 12 minutes. Turn the cooked rice out on to a tray and leave to cool.

2 Using a sharp knife, thinly slice the beef.

3 Mix together the soy sauce, tomato ketchup and Thai seven spice seasoning. Spoon this mixture over the beef and toss well to coat evenly.

4 Heat the groundnut oil in a large preheated wok.

5 Add the beef to the wok and stir-fry for 3–4 minutes.

6 Add the onion, carrots and peas to the wok and stir-fry for a further 2–3 minutes.

7 Add the cooked rice to the wok and stir to combine.

8 Beat the eggs with 2 tablespoons of cold water. Drizzle the egg mixture over the rice and stir-fry for 3–4 minutes,

or until the rice is heated through and the egg has set.

9 Transfer to a warm serving bowl and serve immediately.

VARIATION

You can use pork fillet or chicken instead of the beef, if you prefer.

Stir-Fried Rice with Chinese Sausage

This is a very quick rice dish as it uses pre-cooked rice. It is therefore ideal when time is short or for a quick lunch-time dish.

Serves 4

INGREDIENTS

350 g/12 oz Chinese sausage
2 tbsp sunflower oil
2 tbsp soy sauce
1 onion, sliced

175 g/6 oz carrots, cut into thin
  sticks
175 g/6 oz/1^1/$_4$ cups peas
100 g/3^1/$_2$ oz/^{3}/$_4$ cup canned
  pineapple cubes, drained

275 g/9^1/$_2$ oz/4^3/$_4$ cups cooked long-
  grain rice
1 egg, beaten
1 tbsp chopped fresh parsley

1 Using a sharp knife, thinly slice the Chinese sausage.

2 Heat the sunflower oil in a large preheated wok.

3 Add the sausage to the wok and stir-fry for 5 minutes.

4 Stir in the soy sauce and allow to bubble for 2–3 minutes, or until syrupy.

5 Add the onion, carrots, peas and pineapple to the wok and stir-fry for a further 3 minutes.

6 Add the cooked rice to the ingredients in the wok and stir-fry for 2–3 minutes, or until the rice is completely heated through.

7 Drizzle the beaten egg over the top of the rice and cook, tossing the ingredients in the wok, until the egg sets.

8 Transfer the stir-fried rice to a large, warm serving bowl and scatter with plenty of chopped fresh parsley. Serve immediately.

COOK'S TIP

Cook extra rice and freeze it in prepration for some of the other rice dishes included in this book as it saves time and enables a meal to be prepared in minutes.

Chinese Risotto

Risotto is a creamy Italian dish made with arborio or risotto rice.
This Chinese version is simply delicious!

Serves 4

INGREDIENTS

2 tbsp groundnut oil
1 onion, sliced
2 cloves garlic, crushed
1 tsp Chinese five spice powder

225 g/8 oz Chinese sausage, sliced
225 g/8 oz carrots, diced
1 green (bell) pepper, deseeded and
  diced

275 g/9^1/$_2$ oz/1^1/$_3$ cups risotto rice
850 ml/1^1/$_2$ pint/1^3/$_4$ cups vegetable
  or chicken stock
1 tbsp fresh chives, snipped

1 Heat the groundnut oil in a large preheated wok.

2 Add the onion, garlic and Chinese five spice powder to the wok and stir-fry for 1 minute.

3 Add the Chinese sausage, carrots and green (bell) pepper to the wok and stir to combine.

4 Stir in the risotto rice and cook for 1 minute.

5 Gradually add the stock, a little at a time, stirring constantly until the liquid has

been completely absorbed and the rice grains are tender.

6 Stir the snipped fresh chives into the wok with the last of the stock.

7 Transfer the Chinese risotto to warm serving bowls and serve immediately.

COOK'S TIP

Chinese sausage is highly flavoured and is made from chopped pork fat, pork meat and spices.

VARIATION

Use a spicy Portuguese sausage if Chinese sausage is unavailable.

Crab Congee

This is a typical Chinese breakfast dish, but it would probably not go down too well at a Western table at this time of day! However, it would be welcomed as a lunch or supper dish as it tastes delicious!

Serves 4

INGREDIENTS

225 g/8 oz/1 cup short-grain rice
1.5 litres/2³/₄ pints/6¹/₄ cups fish
   stock

¹/₂ tsp salt
100 g/3¹/₂ oz Chinese sausage, thinly
   sliced

225 g/8 oz white crab meat
6 spring onions (scallions), sliced
2 tbsp chopped coriander (cilantro)

1 Place the short-grain rice in a large preheated wok.

2 Add the fish stock to the wok and bring to the boil. Reduce the heat, then simmer gently for 1 hour, stirring the mixture from time to time.

3 Add the salt, Chinese sausage, crab meat, spring onions (scallions) and coriander (cilantro) to the wok and heat through for about 5 minutes.

4 Add a little more water if the congee "porridge" is too thick.

5 Transfer the crab congee to warm serving bowls and serve immediately.

COOK'S TIP

Always buy the freshest possible crab meat; fresh is best, although frozen or canned will work for this recipe. The delicate, sweet flavour of crab diminishes quickly: this is why many Chinese cooks make a point of buying live crabs. In the West, crabs are almost always sold ready-cooked. The crab should feel heavy for its size, and when it is shaken, there should be no sound of water inside.

COOK'S TIP

Short-grain rice absorbs liquid more slowly than long-grain rice and therefore gives a different textured dish. A risotto rice, such as arborio, would also be ideal for this recipe.

Chicken Chow Mein

No noodle section of an Oriental book would be complete without a Chow Mein *recipe. This classic dish requires no introduction as it is already a favourite amongst most Chinese food-eaters.*

Serves 4

INGREDIENTS

250 g/9 oz packet of medium egg noodles
2 tbsp sunflower oil
275 g/9 1/2 oz cooked chicken breasts, shredded

1 clove garlic, finely chopped
1 red (bell) pepper, deseeded and thinly sliced
100 g/3 1/2 oz shiitake mushrooms, sliced

6 spring onions (scallions), sliced
100 g/3 1/2 oz/1 cup beansprouts
3 tbsp soy sauce
1 tbsp sesame oil

1 Place the egg noodles in a large bowl or dish and break them up slightly.

2 Pour enough boiling water over the noodles to cover and leave to stand whilst preparing the other ingredients.

3 Heat the sunflower oil in a large preheated wok.

4 Add the shredded chicken, finely chopped garlic, (bell) pepper slices, mushrooms, spring onions (scallions) and beansprouts

to the wok and stir-fry for about 5 minutes.

5 Drain the noodles thoroughly. Add the noodles to the wok, toss well and stir-fry for a further 5 minutes.

6 Drizzle the soy sauce and sesame oil over the chow mein and toss until well combined.

7 Transfer the chicken chow mein to warm serving bowls and serve immediately.

VARIATION

You can make the chow mein with a selection of vegetables for a vegetarian dish, if you prefer.

Egg Noodles with Chicken & Oyster Sauce

The chicken and noodles are cooked and then a flavoured egg mixture is tossed into the dish to coat the noodles and meat in this delicious recipe.

Serves 4

INGREDIENTS

250 g/9 oz egg noodles
450 g/1 lb chicken thighs

2 tbsp groundnut oil
100 g/3¹/2 oz carrots, sliced

3tbsp oyster sauce
2 eggs
3 tbsp cold water

1 Place the egg noodles in a large bowl or dish. Pour enough boiling water over the noodles to cover and leave to stand for 10 minutes.

2 Meanwhile, remove the skin from the chicken thighs. Cut the chicken flesh into small pieces, using a sharp knife.

3 Heat the groundnut oil in a large preheated wok.

4 Add the pieces of chicken and the carrot slices to the wok and stir-fry the mixture for about 5 minutes.

5 Drain the noodles thoroughly. Add the noodles to the wok and stir-fry for a further 2–3 minutes or until the noodles are heated through.

6 Beat together the oyster sauce, eggs and 3 tablespoons of cold water. Drizzle the mixture over the noodles and stir-fry for a further 2–3 minutes or until the eggs set. Transfer to warm serving bowls and serve hot.

VARIATION

Flavour the eggs with soy sauce or hoisin sauce as an alternative to the oyster sauce, if you prefer.

Ginger Chilli Beef with Crispy Noodles

Crispy noodles are terrific and may also be served on their own as a side dish, sprinkled with sugar and salt. Here they are complemented by the gingered chilli beef.

Serves 4

INGREDIENTS

225 g/8 oz medium egg noodles
350 g/12 oz beef fillet
2 tbsp sunflower oil
1 tsp ground ginger
1 clove garlic, crushed

1 red chilli, deseeded and very finely
  chopped
100 g/3½ oz carrots, cut into thin
  sticks
6 spring onions (scallions), sliced

2 tbsp lime marmalade
2 tbsp soy sauce
oil, for frying

1 Place the noodles in a large dish or bowl. Pour over enough boiling water to cover the noodles and leave to stand for about 10 minutes while you stir-fry the rest of the ingredients.

2 Using a sharp knife, thinly slice the beef.

3 Heat the sunflower oil in a large preheated wok.

4 Add the beef and ginger to the wok and stir-fry for about 5 minutes.

5 Add the garlic, chilli, carrots and spring onions (scallions) to the wok and stir-fry for a further 2–3 minutes.

6 Add the lime marmalade and soy sauce to the wok and allow to bubble for 2 minutes. Remove the chilli beef and ginger mixture, set aside and keep warm.

7 Heat the oil for frying in the wok.

8 Drain the noodles thoroughly and pat dry with absorbent

kitchen paper. Carefully lower the noodles into the hot oil and cook for 2–3 minutes or until crispy. Drain the noodles on absorbent kitchen paper.

9 Divide the noodles between 4 serving plates and top with the chilli beef and ginger mixture. Serve immediately.

VARIATION

Use pork or chicken instead of the beef, if you prefer.

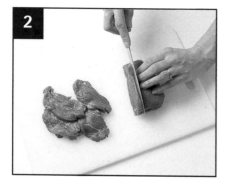

Twice-cooked Lamb with Noodles

Here lamb is first boiled and then fried with soy sauce, oyster sauce and spinach
and finally tossed with noodles for a richly flavoured dish.

Serves 4

INGREDIENTS

250 g/9 oz packet egg noodles
450 g/1 lb lamb loin fillet, thinly
sliced

2 tbsp soy sauce
2 tbsp sunflower oil
2 cloves garlic, crushed

1 tbsp caster (superfine) sugar
2 tbsp oyster sauce
175 g/6 oz baby spinach

1 Place the egg noodles in a large bowl and cover with boiling water. Leave to soak for about 10 minutes.

2 Bring a large saucepan of water to the boil. Add the lamb and cook for 5 minutes. Drain thoroughly.

3 Place the slices of lamb in a bowl and mix with the soy sauce and 1 tablespoon of the sunflower oil.

4 Heat the remaining sunflower oil in a large preheated wok.

5 Add the marinated lamb and garlic to the wok and stir-fry for about 5 minutes or until just beginning to brown.

6 Add the caster (superfine) sugar and oyster sauce to the wok and stir to combine.

7 Drain the noodles thoroughly. Add the noodles to the wok and stir-fry for a further 5 minutes.

8 Add the spinach to the wok and cook for 1 minute or until the leaves just wilt. Transfer the lamb and noodles to serving bowls and serve hot.

COOK'S TIP

If using dried noodles, follow the instructions on the packet as they require less soaking.

Singapore-style Prawn (Shrimp) Noodles

Singapore noodles are a classic dish and can be served as a main meal or as an accompaniment. This dish combines meat, vegetables, prawns (shrimp) and noodles in a curried coconut sauce.

Serves 4

INGREDIENTS

250 g/9 oz thin rice noodles
4 tbsp groundnut oil
2 cloves garlic, crushed
2 red chillies, deseeded and very
   finely chopped
1 tsp grated fresh ginger
2 tbsp Madras curry paste
2 tbsp rice wine vinegar

1 tbsp caster (superfine) sugar
225 g/8 oz cooked ham, finely
   shredded
100 g/3^1/$_2$ oz/1^1/$_4$ cups canned
   waterchestnuts, sliced
100 g/3^1/$_2$ oz mushrooms, sliced
100 g/3^1/$_2$ oz/^{3}/$_4$ cup peas

1 red (bell) pepper, deseeded and
   thinly sliced
100 g/3^1/$_2$ oz peeled prawns (shrimp)
2 large eggs
4 tbsp coconut milk
25 g/1 oz/^{1}/$_4$ cup desiccated
   (shredded) coconut
2 tbsp chopped fresh coriander
   (cilantro)

1 Place the rice noodles in a large bowl, cover with boiling water and leave to soak for about 10 minutes. Drain the noodles thoroughly, then toss them with 2 tablespoons of groundnut oil.

2 Heat the remaining groundnut oil in a large preheated wok. Add the garlic, chillies, ginger, curry paste, wine vinegar and sugar to the wok and stir-fry for 1 minute.

3 Add the ham, waterchestnuts, mushrooms, peas and red (bell) pepper to the wok and stir-fry for 5 minutes.

4 Add the noodles and prawns (shrimps) to the wok and stir-fry for 2 minutes.

5 Beat together the eggs and coconut milk. Drizzle the mixture into the wok and stir-fry until the egg sets.

6 Add the desiccated (shredded) coconut and chopped coriander (cilantro) to the wok and toss to combine. Transfer the noodles to warm serving dishes and serve immediately.

VARIATION

Egg noodles may be used instead of rice noodles, if preferred.

Sweet & Sour Noodles

This is a delicious Thai dish which combines sweet and sour flavours with the addition of egg, rice noodles, large prawns (shrimp) and vegetables for a real treat.

Serves 4

INGREDIENTS

3 tbsp fish sauce

2 tbsp distilled white vinegar

2 tbsp caster (superfine) or palm sugar

2 tbsp tomato purée

2 tbsp sunflower oil

3 cloves garlic, crushed

350 g/12 oz rice noodles, soaked in boiling water for 5 minutes

8 spring onions (scallions), sliced

175 g/6 oz carrot, grated

150 g/5^1/$_2$ oz/1^1/$_4$ cups beansprouts

2 eggs, beaten

225 g/8 oz peeled king prawns (shrimp)

50 g/1^3/$_4$ oz/^{1}/$_2$ cup chopped peanuts

1 tsp chilli flakes, to garnish

1 Mix together the fish sauce, vinegar, sugar and tomato purée in a small bowl. Set aside until required.

2 Heat the sunflower oil in a large preheated wok.

3 Add the garlic to the wok and stir-fry for 30 seconds.

4 Drain the noodles thoroughly and add them to the wok together with the fish sauce and tomato purée mixture. Mix well to combine.

5 Add the spring onions (scallions), carrot and beansprouts to the wok and stir-fry for 2–3 minutes.

6 Move the contents of the wok to one side, add the beaten eggs to the empty part of the wok and cook until the egg sets. Add the noodles, prawns (shrimp) and peanuts to the wok and toss together until well combined.

7 Transfer to warm serving dishes and garnish with chilli flakes. Serve hot.

COOK'S TIP

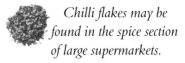

Chilli flakes may be found in the spice section of large supermarkets.

Noodles with Chilli & Prawn (Shrimp)

This is a simple dish to prepare and is packed with flavour,
making it an ideal choice for special occasions.

Serves 4

INGREDIENTS

250 g/9 oz thin glass noodles
2 tbsp sunflower oil
1 onion, sliced
2 red chillies, deseeded and very
  finely chopped

4 lime leaves, thinly shredded
1 tbsp fresh coriander (cilantro)
2 tbsp palm or caster (superfine)
  sugar
2 tbsp fish sauce

450 g/1 lb raw tiger prawns (large
  shrimp), peeled

1 Place the noodles in a large bowl. Pour over enough boiling water to cover the noodles and leave to stand for 5 minutes. Drain the noodles thoroughly.

2 Heat the sunflower oil in a large preheated wok.

3 Add the onion, chillies and lime leaves to the wok and stir-fry for 1 minute.

4 Add the coriander (cilantro), palm or caster (superfine) sugar, fish sauce and prawns (shrimp) to the wok and stir-fry for a further 2 minutes or until the prawns (shrimp) turn pink.

5 Add the drained noodles to the wok, toss to mix well, and stir-fry for 1–2 minutes or until heated through.

6 Transfer to warm serving bowls and serve immediately.

COOK'S TIP

Fish sauce is an essential staple throughout Thailand. You will usually find this labelled as nam pla.

COOK'S TIP

If you cannot buy raw tiger prawns (large shrimp), use cooked prawns (shrimp) instead and cook them with the noodles for 1 minute only, just to heat through.

Stir-Fried Cod & Mango with Noodles

*Fish and fruit are tossed with a trio of (bell) peppers in this spicy dish
served with noodles for a quick, healthy meal.*

Serves 4

INGREDIENTS

250 g/9 oz packet egg noodles
450 g/1 lb skinless cod fillet
1 tbsp paprika
2 tbsp sunflower oil
1 red onion, sliced

1 orange (bell) pepper, deseeded and
  sliced
1 green (bell) pepper, deseeded and
  sliced
100 g/3^1/2 oz baby corn cobs, halved

1 mango, sliced
100 g/3^1/2 oz/1 cup beansprouts
2 tbsp tomato ketchup
2 tbsp soy sauce
2 tbsp medium sherry
1 tsp cornflour (cornstarch)

1 Place the egg noodles in a large bowl and cover with boiling water. Leave to stand for about 10 minutes.

2 Rinse the cod fillet and pat dry with absorbent kitchen paper. Using a sharp knife, cut the cod flesh into thin strips.

3 Place the cod in a large bowl Add the paprika and toss well to combine.

4 Heat the sunflower oil in a large preheated wok.

5 Add the onion, (bell) peppers and baby corn cobs to the wok and stir-fry for about 5 minutes.

6 Add the cod to the wok together with the mango and stir-fry for a further 2–3 minutes or until the fish is tender.

7 Add the beansprouts to the wok and toss well to combine.

8 Mix together the tomato ketchup, soy sauce , sherry and cornflour (cornstarch). Add

the mixture to the wok and cook, stirring occasionally, until the juices thicken.

9 Drain the noodles thoroughly and transfer to serving bowls. Transfer the cod and mango stir-fry to separate serving bowls and serve immediately.

VARIATION

Use other white fish, such as monkfish or haddock, instead of the cod, if you prefer.

Japanese Noodles with Spicy Vegetables

*These noodles are highly spiced with chilli and flavoured
with sesame seeds for a nutty taste which is a true delight.*

Serves 4

INGREDIENTS

450 g/1 lb fresh Japanese noodles
1 tbsp sesame oil
1 tbsp sesame seeds
1 tbsp sunflower oil

1 red onion, sliced
100 g/3$\frac{1}{2}$ oz mangetout, (snow peas)
175 g/6 oz carrots, thinly sliced
350 g/12 oz white cabbage, shredded

3 tbsp sweet chilli sauce
2 spring onions (scallions), sliced,
  to garnish

1 Bring a large saucepan of water to the boil. Add the Japanese noodles to the pan and cook for 2–3 minutes. Drain the noodles thoroughly.

2 Toss the noodles with the sesame oil and sesame seeds.

3 Heat the sunflower oil in a large preheated wok.

4 Add the onion slices, mangetout (snow peas), carrot slices and shredded cabbage to the wok and stir-fry for about 5 minutes.

5 Add the sweet chilli sauce to the wok and cook, stirring occasionally, for a further 2 minutes.

6 Add the sesame noodles to the wok, toss well to combine and heat through for a further 2–3 minutes. (You may wish to serve the noodles separately, so transfer them to the serving bowls.)

7 Transfer the Japanese noodles and spicy vegetables to warm serving bowls and garnish with sliced spring onions (scallions). Serve immediately.

COOK'S TIP

If fresh Japanese noodles are difficult to get hold of, use dried rice noodles or thin egg noodles instead.

Stir-Fried Rice Noodles with Green Beans & Coconut Sauce

These rice noodles and vegetables are tossed in a crunchy peanut and chilli sauce for a quick satay-flavoured recipe.

Serves 4

INGREDIENTS

275 g/10 oz rice sticks (wide, flat rice noodles)
3 tbsp groundnut oil
2 cloves garlic, crushed
2 shallots, sliced

225 g/8 oz green beans, sliced
100 g/3³/4 oz cherry tomatoes, halved
1 tsp chilli flakes
4 tbsp crunchy peanut butter
150 ml/¼ pint/²/3 cup coconut milk

1 tbsp tomato purée
sliced spring onions (scallions), to garnish

1 Place the rice sticks (wide, flat rice noodles) in a large bowl and pour over enough boiling water to cover. Leave to stand for 10 minutes.

2 Heat the groundnut oil in a large preheated wok.

3 Add the garlic and shallots and stir-fry for 1 minute.

4 Drain the rice sticks (wide, flat rice noodles) thoroughly.

5 Add the green beans and drained noodles to the wok and stir-fry for 5 minutes.

6 Add the cherry tomatoes to the wok and mix well.

7 Mix together the chilli flakes, peanut butter, coconut milk and tomato purée.

8 Pour the chilli mixture over the noodles, toss well to combine and heat through.

9 Transfer to warm serving dishes and garnish with spring onion (scallion) slices. Serve immediately.

VARIATION

Add slices of chicken or beef to the recipe and stir-fry with the beans and noodles in step 5 for a more substantial main meal.

Noodle & Mango Salad

Fruit combines well with the peanut dressing, (bell) peppers and chilli in this delicous hot salad.

Serves 4

INGREDIENTS

250 g/9 oz thread egg noodles
2 tbsp groundnut oil
4 shallots, sliced
2 cloves garlic, crushed
1 red chilli, deseeded and sliced

1 red (bell) pepper, deseeded and sliced
1 green (bell) pepper, deseeded and sliced
1 ripe mango, sliced into thin strips

25 g/1 oz/¼ cup salted peanuts, chopped
4 tbsp peanut butter
100 ml/3½ fl oz/⅓ cup coconut milk
1 tbsp tomato purée

1 Place the egg noodles in a large dish or bowl. Pour over enough boiling water to cover the noodles and leave to stand for 10 minutes.

2 Heat the groundnut oil in a large preheated wok.

3 Add the shallots, garlic, chilli and (bell) pepper slices to the wok and stir-fry for 2–3 minutes.

4 Drain the egg noodles thoroughly.

5 Add the drained noodles and mango slices to the wok and heat through for about 2 minutes.

6 Transfer the noodle and mango salad to warmed serving dishes and scatter with chopped peanuts.

7 Mix together the peanut butter, coconut milk and tomato purée until well combined and then spoon over the noodle salad as a dressing. Serve immediately.

COOK'S TIP

If preferred, gently heat the peanut dressing before pouring over the noodle salad.

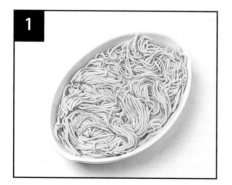

Index

Asparagus & red (bell) pepper parcels 184
aubergines (eggplants):
seven spice aubergines (eggplants) 24
spiced stir-fry 210

Beef:
chilli beef stir-fry salad 84
egg fried rice with seven spice beef 226
ginger chilli beef 238
marinated beef stir-fry 86
stir-fried garlic beef 94
stir-fried vegetables & 82
stir-fried with baby onions & palm sugar 88
sweet potato stir-fry 90
with green peas & black bean sauce 92
broccoli & Chinese leaves with black bean sauce 196
butternut squash stir-fried with cashew nuts 200

Carrot & orange stir-fry 186
cauliflower & coriander (cilantro) stir-fry 194
chicken:
chicken, (bell) pepper & orange stir-fry 52
chicken, spring green & yellow bean stir-fry 50
Chinese chicken rice 222
chow mein 234
coconut chicken curry 54
egg noodles with 236
honey & soy stir-fried chicken 66
peppered stir-fry 64
spicy noodle soup 8
stir-fried garlic chicken 72
stir-fried ginger chicken 48
stir-fried onion rice with five spice chicken 220
stir-fried with cashew nuts & yellow bean sauce 68
stir-fried with chilli & crispy basil 70
stir-fried with cumin seeds & aubergine (eggplant) 74
stir-fried with lemon & sesame seeds 60
stir-fry with cumin seeds 58
sweet & sour chicken 56
Thai red chicken 62
chilli corn balls, deep-fried 182
chilli fish soup 16
Chinese leaves with shiitake mushrooms & crab meat 152
chow mein, chicken 234
coconut: & crab soup 14
prawns (shrimp) 140

cod:
chilli fish soup 16
fried fish with coconut & basil 138
stir-fried cod & mango 132, 248
Thai-style fish cakes 32
courgettes (zucchini), deep-fried 180
crab: Chinese leaves with shiitake mushrooms & 152
coconut & crab soup 14
crab & sweetcorn noodle soup 10
crab congee 232
stir-fried with chilli 150

Duck:
hoisin duck with leek & stir-fried cabbage 76
with baby corn cobs & pineapple 78

Fish cakes, Thai-style 32
fish fillets, braised 136

Green beans, stir-fried with lettuce 178

Lamb:
curried stir-fried lamb 114
garlic-infused lamb 116
spring onion (scallion) & lamb stir-fry 112
stir-fried with black bean sauce 110
stir-fried with orange 120
Thai-style lamb 118
twice-cooked lamb 240
with satay sauce 108
leeks with baby corn cobs & yellow bean sauce 204
lettuce, stir-fried with mussels & lemon grass 154
liver: lamb's liver with green (bell) peppers 122
spicy chicken livers 30

Monkfish:
stir-fried gingered 134
mushrooms:
Chinese mushrooms with deep-fried tofu (bean curd) 198
hot & sour soup 18
spinach stir-fry with shiitake & honey 188
stir-fried Japanese mushroom noodles 170
mussels:
in black bean sauce with spinach 156
stir-fried lettuce with 154

Noodles 215, 234-54
chicken chow mein 234
egg noodles with chicken & oyster sauce 236
ginger chilli beef with crispy noodles 238
Japanese noodles with spicy vegetables 250
noodle & mango salad 254
noodles with chilli & prawn (shrimp) 246
Singapore-style prawn (shrimp) noodles 242
stir-fried cod & mango with 248
stir-fried Japanese mushroom noodles 170
stir-fried rice noodles with green beans 252
sweet & sour noodles 244
twice-cooked lamb with 240

Omelette, prawn (shrimp) 42, 142
oysters, stir-fried with tofu (bean curd) 162

Pak choi:
crispy seaweed 28
stir-fried with red onion & cashew nuts 174
peppers (bell):
stir-fried (bell) pepper trio 208
pork:
Chinese five spice crispy pork 98
pork fillet stir-fry 96
spicy pork balls 100
sweet & sour pork 102
sweet chilli pork fried rice 224
twice-cooked pork with (bell) peppers 104
with mooli (white radish) 106
prawns (shrimp):
Chinese prawn (shrimp) salad 38
coconut prawns (shrimp) 140
crispy chilli & peanut prawns (shrimp) 34
noodles with chilli & 246
prawn (shrimp) omelette 42, 142
prawn (shrimp) parcels 36
salt & pepper prawns (shrimp) 44
sesame prawn (shrimp) toasts 40
Singapore-style noodles 242
spicy Thai soup with 12
vegetables with egg & 148
with crispy ginger 146
with spicy tomatoes 144

Quorn with ginger & mixed vegetables 202

Rice 215-32
Chinese chicken rice 222
Chinese risotto 230
Chinese vegetable rice 190
coconut rice 218
crab congee 232
egg fried rice with seven spice beef 226
fried rice with spicy beans 216
stir-fried onion rice 220
stir-fried rice with Chinese sausage 228
sweet chilli pork fried rice 224

Salads 38, 254
salmon:
stir-fried with pineapple 128
teriyaki stir-fried 126
sausage: stir-fried rice with Chinese sausage 228
scallops: pancakes 158
seared scallops with butter sauce 160
seaweed, crispy 28
Singapore-style prawn (shrimp) noodles 242
soups 7-18
spinach stir-fry with shiitake & honey 188
spring rolls, vegetable 22
squid: crispy fried 164
stir-fried with green (bell) peppers 166
sweet potato stir-fry 90
sweetcorn: deep-fried chilli corn balls 182
Thai-style spicy fritters 20

Tofu (bean curd):
Chinese mushrooms with 198
stir-fried with peanut & chilli sauce 26
with soy sauce & green (bell) peppers 176
tuna & vegetable stir-fry 130
turkey, stir-fried with cranberry glaze 80

Vegetables:
Chinese vegetable rice 190
stir-fried with peanuts & eggs 212
stir-fried with sherry & soy sauce 172
vegetable stir-fry 206
vegetable stir-fry with hoisin sauce 192
with prawns (shrimp) & egg 148

Index compiled by Hilary Bird.